Developing Educational Hypermedia: Coordination and Reuse

Printed in the United States of America

Library of Congress Cataloging-in-Publication Data
Rada, R. (Roy), 1951–
    Developing educational hypermedia. : coordination and reuse / Roy
Rada
        p. cm. — (Tutorial monographs in artificial intelligence)
    Includes bibliographical references and index
    ISBN 1-56750-215-6. — ISBN 1-56750-216-4 (pbk.)
    1. Computer-assisted instruction. 2. Interactive multimedia.
3. Educational technology. 4. Hypertext systems. 5. Interactive
multimedia. I. Title. II. Series.
LB1028.46.R317   1996
371.3'34—dc20   95-25647
                                                               CIP

Ablex Publishing Corporation
355 Chestnut Street
Norwood, New Jersey 07648

Table of Contents

Preface

As technology improves, people look to ways to utilize it to their advantage. This process often has a profound effect on the *work process,* as new skills have to be learned and old ones become redundant. One of the areas of striking development is in the provision of tools to assist the learner and the educator.

Interactive multimedia or hypermedia is one of the technologies which is most influencing the educating and training of people. Unlike the printed word which could in many ways be readily produced by a lone individual, hypermedia development often involves a *team* of professionals.

The term educational interactive multimedia is a mouthful. Common synonyms to it might be computer-based teaching material or computer-based learning material. Within some subcultures the term *courseware* is synonymous with educational interactive multimedia and for the benefit of its shortness the term courseware is often used in this book.

This book shows how coordination and reuse pertain to the development of courseware. Skills of a teacher, an artist, a software engineer, and more must be combined to produce effective courseware. *Courseware development* provides new opportunities and challenges to researchers, practitioners, and designers from a number of disciplines such as computer science, education, library science, communication, art, psychology, sociology, and management. Slightly different sets of courseware are required for various potential audiences within the same subject sphere, allowing reuse of existing material, but libraries of reusable courseware are largely missing. Advanced network techniques provide extended communication capabilities, but conceptual frameworks which can be directly applied to the coordinated development of courseware are largely missing. Models must be developed to guide the courseware authoring process — both the reuse of courseware and the coordination of authors.

Coordination and reuse are critical to the future of courseware development. To effectively handle dependencies between people decisions have to be made, so *coordination* involves decision making, which in turn involves communication and a common language. Through *reuse* an organization can benefit from the material which it has either itself created in the past or has acquired from somewhere else.

This book has 3 top-level parts: Part I "Basics", Part II "Examples", and Part III "Systems". Basics includes 3 chapters entitled 'Educational Hypermedia', 'Coordination, and Reuse'. Examples contains two chapters entitled 'University

Examples' and 'Commercial Examples', while Systems has two chapters entitled 'University Systems' and 'Commercial Systems'. University and commercial experiences are contrasted to show where the strengths of one can apply to the other.

This book is partially based on work in the Commission of the European Communities project called Open Systems for Collaborative Authoring and Reuse (OSCAR) of Courseware. The Prime Contractor of the OSCAR project was Tecnopolis Csata Novus Ortus in Bari, Italy and Antonio Ulloa at Tecnopolis was the Project Coordinator. Several people from Tecnopolis contributed to the chapter 'Commercial System'. The chapter 'Commercial Examples' was partially extracted from a document prepared by the OSCAR partner FIAR in Milan, Italy under the leadership of Emilio Bernasconi.

Many people from the 'Many Using and Creating Hypermedia' (MUCH) team at the University of Liverpool contributed to this book. Chaomei Chen and Antonios Michailidis helped write the chapter on Coordination. Sharon Acquah's description of her courseware reuse system and Denise McDonough's review of courseware development practices at the University of Liverpool found their way into the book, as has Pelaga-Irene Gouma's and Anthony Deakin's study of the MUCH team itself. Claude Ghaoui helped manage the editing of the book. Renata Malinowski did the subediting. Helen Forster typeset the final copy of the book.

Many influences beyond those of the OSCAR and MUCH projects might be credited. The most salient of these would be Mary Hopper's Ph.D thesis entitled *Courseware Projects in Advanced Educational Computing Environments* which provided much of the material in the chapter 'University Examples'. Most generally, the pupils and educators world-wide with their interest in innovative methods and tools for learning are responsible for this book.

Part I: Basics

What is *educational hypermedia?* How do people work together? And what is required to successfully reuse information? These questions are answered in the next three chapters in preparation for Parts II and III in which examples of and systems for educational hypermedia development are presented.

1
Educational Hypermedia

People use technology because technology can do certain necessary or desirable tasks more *effectively* or *efficiently* than people. Technology can also permit people to do things which were not previously possible. Educational technology can help people effectively and efficiently teach or learn, and furthermore it supports new types of teaching and learning.

Educational technology can take many forms, such as:

- an overhead projector for showing transparencies to students,
- a television for broadcasting educational movies,
- a computer program to provide multiple choice questions to students, and
- a televideo conference facility through which geographically separated individuals might interact and learn.

This book will focus on the latest developments in technology, such as those indicated by the computer program and the televideo conference. Such technology will in this book be called *educational hypermedia technology*. A term which will be used in this book as a synonym to educational hypermedia technology is *courseware*. Courseware has been defined as 'computer programs intended to deliver some type of instruction' [116] but in this book means 'hypermedia intended to deliver some type of instruction'. The rest of this chapter makes clear the meaning of hypermedia. One should note that many other terms, such as *computer-assisted learning, computer-based teaching,* and *computer-assisted instruction,* have been used by those who work with educational hypermedia. This book will attempt to focus on the terms educational hypermedia or courseware, but the reader should recognize that these different terms are typically used to mean more or less the same thing.

In the newspapers and on television one can learn about the new media — the terms *hypertext, multimedia,* and *hypermedia* are widely used but frequently misunderstood. This chapter proposes clear distinctions. The primary distinction is between the links of hypertext and the timing of multimedia. Hypermedia involves both linking and timing [115].

Many other terms need to be finely distinguished. One such distinction is between a *system* and the *information* which the system delivers. Thus a hypertext (multimedia or hypermedia) system is for producing and delivering hypertext (multimedia or hypermedia). Another important distinction is between creating information versus accessing information.

One of the most popular new information systems is the *World Wide Web*. In the early 1990s the amount of traffic on the World Wide Web increased at an exponential rate [9]. The system supports links among files, and the files may contain various media. Does the World Wide Web offer hypertext, multimedia, or hypermedia (see Figure 1.1)?

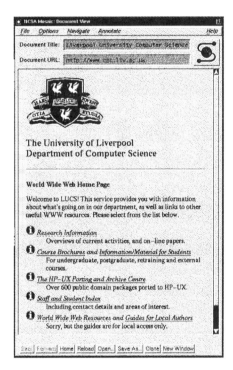

Figure 1.1: *A World Wide Web Page*: In this example of accessing the World Wide Web from the University of Liverpool, underlined terms can be selected by the user, and the system will then follow a link to another file.

1.1 Hypertext

Hypertext can be described as text with links among the components, and a hypertext system provides a mechanism for moving along the links [109]. The modern history of hypertext is often traced to Vannevar Bush. During the Second World War Vannevar Bush directed the American Office of Scientific Research and Development and coordinated the activities of 6,000 American scientists in the application of science to warfare and the development of the nuclear bomb. He wanted to also apply science to peaceful purposes and proposed a technological solution to the information explosion problem in the shape of a device he termed the Memex (Memory Extender) [92]. This was a device in which an individual stores all his items of information in miniaturized form on film and which allows for the linking of one item to another. A machine then allows the reader to view the film, point to links, and readily retrieve further film. Memex would provide for associative indexing "whereby any item may be caused at will to select immediately and automatically another."

1.1.1   Hypertext Models

Formal models of hypertext may emphasize clear, systematic relationships between structure and function. Numerous models of hypertext have been developed and essentially all of these emphasize the notion of nodes and links [75]. The most popular of such models was developed at a meeting in a city called Dexter and is called the *Dexter hypertext model* [54].

In the Dexter model, hypertext has a 'runtime layer', a 'storage layer', and a 'within-component layer' [55]. The storage layer is composed of nodes and links. Nodes may be composites of other nodes. Links connect any number of nodes. Each node or link may have arbitrarily many attributes (see Figure 1.2). Between the storage and runtime layers is a 'presentation mechanism' and between the 'storage' and 'within-component' layers is an 'anchoring mechanism' (see Figure 1.3). The presentation mechanism presents the hypertext to the user, and the anchoring mechanism retrieves components.

Link types can be divided into those that connect nodes, those that associate nodes with additional information, and those that invoke programs [11]. *Virtual* and *conditional* links are examples of link types that invoke programs. With virtual links the user specifies the link's start explicitly and gives a description of its destination; the computer then finds some target node which satisfies the description of the destination. An example of a conditional link is if evidence Q is present, then link from node A to node containing Q, otherwise link from the node A to the node containing P [30].

1.1.2   Searching versus Browsing

People may be perceived as *accessing information* in many ways, depending on their goals and the character of the hypertext accessed [24]. These types of access along one dimension may be called searching, browsing, or reading [111]. A question for which one concept is key to the question and that concept occurs just once in the hypertext is a question ideally suited for a search function.

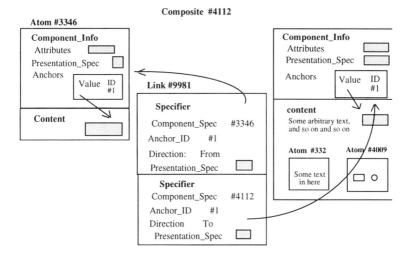

Figure 1.2: *Nodes and Links.* A depiction of overall organization of the storage layer including two nodes: atomic node #3346 and composite node #4412. Link #9981 has an anchor in both nodes.

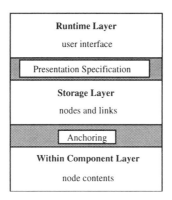

Figure 1.3: *Dexter Model Layers.* The storage layer only provides the mechanisms to organize components (nodes) and links without considering the contents of components, which is the task of the within-component layer. The interface between the storage layer and within-component layer is an anchoring mechanism which is used for addressing locations within a component. The runtime layer focuses on how information is presented to users.

A browse question has several important concepts and they connect to several parts of the hypertext, some of which are relevant and some not. If a few parts of the hypertext must be accessed to handle a task properly and those parts are neatly connected with links in a hypertext network, then *browsing* is appropriate. A table can be arranged which associates an access method with the number of key concepts in the task definition and the number of hypertext parts relevant to the task (see Figure 1.4). Reading is appropriate when many parts and concepts must be considered [151].

concepts in question	relevant items	access method
one	one	search
several	several	browse
many	many	read

Figure 1.4: *Mapping of question, hypertext, and access method.* The left-most column gives the number of concepts in a question, the middle column is the number of items in the hypertext space which must be retrieved to answer the question.

Paper is a powerful medium whose familiarity, tangibility, and portability make it more attractive than computerized information for many understanding tasks [57]. Hypermedia systems are useful for searching tasks, but for browsing only when the links are tuned to a particular task. In some cases, rather than asking whether hypermedia systems will replace paper, one should be looking for the ways in which the two media can complement one another.

1.1.3   Interfaces

The *interface* is critical to the success of a hypertext system [89]. Many papers have been written about the user response to various presentations of hypertext on various tasks. As one surveys these papers, the question continually arises of 'what can be said in the general case'? One particular survey showed most strongly the importance of user types.

In comparing the results of studies on hypertext, the enormous effect of *user age* becomes apparent [90]. Young users found hypertext very attractive, whereas middle-age users were disinclined to use hypertext. The other most significant factor in this survey of hypertext studies was the *motivation of the user*. When the users were highly motivated to perform a certain task, then they contributed much more to the hypertext exercise than did those whose motivation was less. Although this result seems intuitively clear, adequate attention has not been paid to this factor. Hypertext system issues, such as button style or window placement, are often the focus of a research paper, but the biggest differences in the acceptability of a hypertext system are the characteristics of the users themselves.

Although the user characteristics are most important, some general guidelines on *interface design* can be provided. The layout of a hypertext screen should draw attention to important pieces of content, as well as the links [131]. A bold word should not both indicate a link at times but at other times simply indicate an important term. Each link type should have a distinct and standard style [58]. For instance, a link that takes the user to the beginning might consistently be represented with a picture of a house.

With electronic media, it is not automatically apparent how much information is available, how it is structured, and where the reader currently is. The concept of the *fisheye view* is based on the analogy to a fisheye camera lens, which distorts the image so that the nearest objects are seen in detail and distant objects are compressed [40]. In the context of a document, a fisheye view shows full details of the immediate location and outlines of other parts of the document [23]. This simple cognitive model makes the fisheye view attractive [35].

To provide the kinesthetic or tangible feel that people appreciate on paper or in person — person interactions one might exploit space and time metaphors [80]. For instance, a *guided tour* across a town with the help of a map and a tour company suggests the travel metaphor. In an interface that exploits the travel metaphor, guided tours are initiated when the user selects a coach icon labeled with the topic of the tour (see Figure 1.5). The user is then guided round a sequence of presentations on the topic until the tour ends. In experiments contrasting interfaces with and without travel metaphors [56], guided tours allowed more accurate overviews of the available material and resulted in a higher rate of exposure to new rather than repeated information.

1.1.4 Authoring Software Manuals

The creating of hypertext is a challenging task that requires many of the skills of the traditional author [123] plus new skills of a hypertext engineer and artist [105]. This section will not review the full range of approaches to hypertext authoring, but will rather focus on one particular approach; namely, that involving task analysis, as applied to one type of hypertext, namely hypertext software manuals.

In contrast to hypertext developed for students, which emphasizes browsing for learning purposes, commercial hypertext must have a strong task orientation, emphasizing the quick solution of specific user problems [28]. The Computer Systems Operation at Hewlett-Packard has developed a rule-based methodology that ensures a high degree of task orientation [22]. Extensive interviews with Hewlett-Packard managers revealed that they had particular concerns for *liability*. If manual

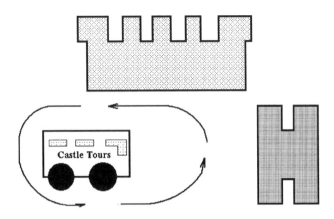

Figure 1.5: *Travel Metaphor.* When the user selects the bus labeled 'Castle Tours', the user is taken to nodes about castles.

users make a serious error, such as deleting all their critical data while following the instructions in the manual, then the company which produced the manual can be sued. Because hypertext may indicate more explicit paths through a text space than a paper document would, the authors have more power to present important paths but also greater risk of providing a path that mistakenly assumes some previous path taken by the user.

Task analysis is an important method in the development of requirements for software that helps ensure that the software will be usable [31]. At Hewlett-Packard the emphasis on usability leads to a stress on task analysis for software development and other kinds of product development as well. In particular, task analysis is the first phase of authoring at Hewlett-Packard.

As a *project* is being developed, writers, together with product engineers and marketing experts, select customers as subjects for a task analysis. These customers are observed either on the job using a current product or in a controlled laboratory setting using a prototype of a new product. For each task, the customer is asked to describe the steps to accomplish it.

Next, technical writers create the hypertext according to a set of rules. One rule states that each primitive task (a task which does not contain any other tasks) must be represented as a separate node. Tasks that are a sequence of primitive tasks must correspond to a path in the hypertext. The authoring process should produce hypertext with an improved degree of *usability*, although testing with users is the only means for verifying usability.

1.2 Multimedia

Multimedia may generally mean any mixture of media but in this book the term refers to the synchronization of time-based media, particularly video and sound (see Figure 1.6) [2]. Although the popularity of multimedia has grown enormously in the 1990s, the *history of multimedia* naturally traces to earlier years. One of the first major engineering accomplishments with combining video and computers was the work of Douglas Engelbart in his Augment system in the mid-1960s [36]. Around the same time, Nicholas Negroponte's Architecture Machine Group developed the Spatial Data Management System which synchronized video screens and other projection devices through joysticks, a touch screen, and stylus. Auditory cues were used to help people navigate in an information space [14].

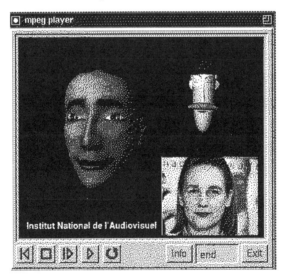

Figure 1.6: *Synchronization with Video* When this video plays the woman's face moves in coordination with the animations. This image was captured from the World Wide Web site http://www.ina.fr/TV/tv_ina.mpg.

1.2.1   Media

A formal communication system consists of an *information source*, an *encoder*, a *communication channel*, a *noise source*, a *decoder*, and a *destination* [128]. A *medium* is the technical or physical means of conveying information along the channel. Information sources may use presentational or representational media to encode a message. Alternately, a message in presentational or representational media may be further encoded by mechanical media (see Figure "Presentational versus Representational Communication"):

- The *presentational media* include the voice and body. The messages encoded via these media are spoken words, gestures, and so on. These are 'acts of communication'.
- The *representational media* include books, paintings, gardening, computer interfaces, and so on. These media make use of cultural conventions to encode a 'message'. They produce 'works of communication'.
- The *mechanical media* include telephones, telexes, computers, and so on. They are transmitters of presentational and representational media.

The presentational and representational media must both come to people via their senses. Text is seen, noise is heard. This may get complicated as, for instance, inscriptions in stone can be both seen and felt. The medium of printed paper may contain pictures, diagrams, and text, all of which are different encodings. Encoded information can itself serve as a base for another medium. For example, in a photograph of a street sign, the base medium is the photograph that carries an image. This image carries the name of the street, represented as text. When media are discussed, the differences between presentational, representational, and mechanical media should be kept in mind.

1.2.2   Time

Time-based media, such as video and audio, may have synchronization requirements [77]. A newscast can be used to illustrate the importance of timing in multimedia. Various presentational and representational media produced with various mechanical means all arrive on the television screen with some critical timing considerations. The storyboard for the newscast might usefully distinguish voice, video, graphics, image, and the newsperson (see Figure 1.8). The importance of the speech being synchronized with the newsperson's mouth movements is just one of the more obvious synchronization requirements.

Data can be *time-dependent* at some times and not at others [18]. For instance, a set of cross-sections of a body is in the first instance related by anatomy or space. If one, however, wanted to present a time-based path through the cross-section, then temporal

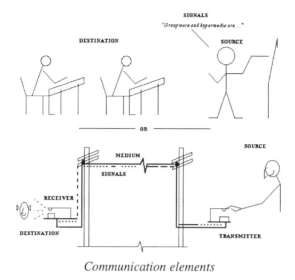

Communication elements

Figure 1.7: *Presentational Versus Representational Communication:* The source is the originator of the message, whereas the destination receives the message. The teacher in the classroom (upper sketch) is using presentational media. In the lower sketch, a mechanical medium carries a message.

connections between the components would be required.

1.2.3   Compression

The *storage space* needed for multimedia may be enormous. One image can require more storage space than an entire book. Video may contain about 30 images per second. Thousands of textbooks without images would occupy no more space than one minute of video.

People do not yet have a standard language for abstracting information from arbitrary images. Methods do, however, exist to *compress* the information in an image. If a large space in the image is of a constant character, then this constancy can be *encoded* so that less space is required to store the image. Later the encoded image may be decoded or decompressed.

Compression and decompression are time consuming operations. One challenge is to compress or decompress information quickly enough so that users will not have to wait for information [8]. Two types of *compression - decompression* relations are the asymmetric and symmetric. Asymmetric relations are those that require frequent use of the decompression process, but for which the compression process is done once and for all at the production of the program. One asymmetric application is the electronic book. Symmetric relations require equal use of the compression and the decompression process. A video conference is a symmetric application.

```
MEDIA                 TIME LINE->
voice          |hello ..............read story
video          |city traffic .......show newsman
graphics       |station logo .................
image          |...............sun rising.....
newsman        |shuffles papers.....read story
```

Figure 1.8: *Newscast and Timing* The different media are in the left-most column and the timeline is on the right. The textual description inside the media-time space shows activity.

1.2.4   Sound

Not until the late 1960s did serious interest in processing *sound* on the computer occur. Sound is, however, for people a fundamental sensory modality. In its raw form, sound is often described in terms of its *frequency* and *amplitude.* The frequency of the sound corresponds to what the person perceives as the sound's pitch. Amplitude corresponds to volume.

Frequency and amplitude for sound are traditionally viewed as continuous or analog phenomenon, but for digital processing this analog sound is sampled. To sample a signal means to examine it at a point in time. From the digital representation that is produced after the sampling, another analog form can be later generated (the same argument applies to video). In principle, one computer could communicate with another, if each computer had *analog-to-digital* and *digital-to-analog* converters. However, with each of these conversions some noise is likely to be introduced. For this and other reasons, ways have been found to encode digital sound so that its storage and transmission from computer to computer can stay in digital form and so that this processing is as economical as possible.

Software exists for manipulating sound in many different ways (see Figure 1.9). The quality of *rendered sound* will depend on the resolution of the sampling and on the accuracy of the compressions/decompressions that have been performed [143]. Sound stored on high quality audio compact disks has been sampled 44 thousand times per second and 16 bits have been used to represent the amplitude of the sound at each instant of sampling. This encoding will require large amounts of space for storage, as a minute of this high quality audio will require well over a megabyte of storage. Much lower rates of sampling and less accurate measurements of amplitude may suffice for many purposes and radically reduce the storage requirements [138].

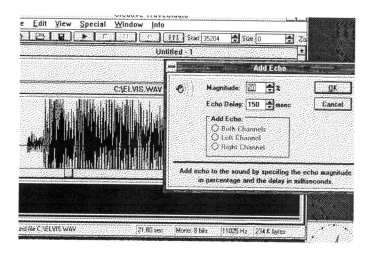

Figure 1.9: *Audio Waveform:* This copy of part of a computer screen shows software that is being used to display the frequency and amplitude of sound that is being played on the audio system connected to the computer. The pop-up window entitled 'Add Echo' allows the user to choose parameters of an echo to add to the sound. In this case the sound that is being played is a recording from Elvis Presley.

1.2.5   Video

During the 1980s standards committees worked to establish uniform approaches to video compression. The *Motion Pictures Experts Group (MPEG)* standard addresses the compression of video and exploits the fact that moving video images change little from frame to frame [85]. Predictive interframe coding is initiated with one coded frame. Each subsequent frame is compared to its predecessor and only the differences between the two are coded.

Video makes enormous demands on a typical computer for memory and speed. Hardware and software are developed to cater to video needs. Microsoft *Video For Windows* (VFW) is a software digital video approach. The default video window is just 160 x 120 pixels. A clip can be viewed (see Figure 1.10) with standard tape transport controls and frame-by-frame controls.

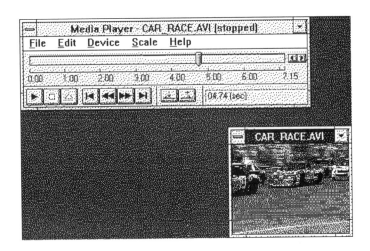

Figure 1.10: *Video for Windows.* The CAR_RACE.AVI clip shown
on these clips lasts 7 seconds and is over 1 megabyte in size.

The *Audio-Video Kernel* (AVK) system addresses the needs of both hardware and
software vendors to support motion video through one, standard, multilayer
architecture [65]. By targeting their applications to the top, software layer of AVK,
software developers are assured of a consistent software environment. In turn,
hardware distributors need only modify the lower, hardware layers of AVK to port it to
their platforms [47].

1.2.6   Multimedia Personal Computer

Few vendors offer an entire multimedia system [149]. To overcome compatibility
problems, several vendors jointly created the *Multimedia Personal Computer* (MPC)
Marketing Council. In 1991 this council consisted of 15 computer-related vendors
and was sponsored by Microsoft. The MPC standard set the minimum standard for
multimedia hardware to run a set of common, multimedia applications.

To the extent that the *MPC standard* survives, it can be expected to undergo continual
evolution. In broad strokes, the 1991 standard included:

•   a midrange microprocessor,

- several megabytes of random access core memory,
- a diskette drive and a large harddisk,
- a Compact Disk - Read Only Memory (CD-ROM) drive,
- audio facilities including microphone input and speaker output,
- high resolution, color graphics,
- serial, parallel, and MIDI ports, and
- the Microsoft Windows operating system.

Windows made the standard workable. For example, any compatible additional hardware for handling sound can be used in a MPC, as long as the vendor writes appropriate Windows software to control the hardware, and all software run under Windows can access that hardware.

Characteristics of the *CD-ROM* of the MPC include [39]:

- High information density — With the density achievable using optical encoding, the disk can contain almost 1 gigabyte of data on a disc less than five inches in diameter.
- Low unit cost — Because disks are manufactured by a well-developed process similar to that used to stamp audio records, unit cost in large quantities is about the same as for an audio record.
- Multimedia storage — Because all CD-ROM data is stored digitally, it is inherently multimedia in that it can store text, images, graphics, sound, and any other information expressed in digital form.

The technology of the CD-ROM is based on small holes burnt into a disk by a laser beam. The CD-ROM cannot be rewritten, whereas magnetic and transistor media can be rewritten many times. The saving grace of CD-ROMs is their low cost [95].

1.3 Hypermedia

The basic support provided by a *hypertext* access system is visiting nodes by traversing links. The user determines how much time to spend at a node and what node to visit next. *Multimedia,* on the other hand, is time-based. Components are meant to be presented in some author-defined, temporal order. The combination of the linking facility associated with hypertext and the synchronization facility of multimedia constitutes *hypermedia* (see Figure 1.11).

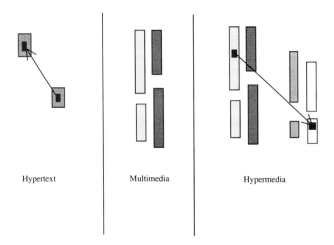

Hypertext   Multimedia   Hypermedia

Figure 1.11: *Hypertext, Multimedia, and Hypermedia.* The leftmost column shows a link from an anchor within one hypertext node to another anchor in another hypertext node. The middle column shows two media types that should begin presentation at the same time with time going from top to bottom. Each media type experiences a delay before resuming but the delays are not at the same time. The rightmost, hypermedia column indicates two multimedia composites and a link from one composite to another.

1.3.1   Links and Timing

To model hypermedia the *Dexter model* (which was presented earlier) for linking is extended to include synchronization capabilities [59]. Temporal relationships may be viewed as those which determine components are presented together and the relative order in which components are presented — these may be called collection and synchronization relations, respectively. The Dexter model provides some support for the collection relation via composite nodes. However, the definition of a composite does not provide a mechanisms for specifying relative timing relationships among the entities of a composite.

Another problem with the hypertext link is that it does not say what happens to the *screen* when the user activates an anchor within a text block. Most systems present a single hypertext node that is either replaced by the destination information or is left on the screen, while another window is provided for the destination information. This is not usually problematic in hypertext because the reader typically will only read one block of text at a time anyhow. For multimedia, however, the presentation of multiple media at the same time may be crucial to the intended meaning and the author must be able to determine what does or does not remain on the screen.

The *Amsterdam Hypermedia Model* (AHM) uses atomic and composite nodes and extends their Dexter model representation [59]. The atomic components of the AHM contain presentation information, component attributes, and link anchor information. The presentation information is expanded from that in the Dexter model to model time-related aspects of the within-component layer. The composite component in the AHM is used to build a presentation structure rather than to simply collect related components for navigation purposes.

CMIFed is a system for creating and accessing hypermedia documents based on the AHM [122]. CMIFed supports a hierarchy view and a channel view. The *hierarchy* view is presented as embedded nodes in a tree-like fashion. Nodes next to each other are started in parallel. Nodes higher in the tree are activated before those lower in the tree (see Figure 1.12). There are three groups of commands: to insert new nodes; to cut and paste nodes; and to display and edit information about nodes, such as the attributes.

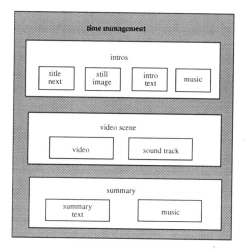

Figure 1.12: *Hierarchy View of CMIFed.* This illustration of how a window of CMIFed appears in the hierarchy view shows the embedded nodes of a presentation about 'time management' that includes text, image, music, video, and sound. Time goes from top to bottom.

The *channel view* shows a transformation of the hierarchy in terms of abstract media channels. This view is presented as a time line, with placement determined automatically by CMIFed. The atomic components are displayed in their own channel along with their precise durations and timing relationships (see Figure 1.13).

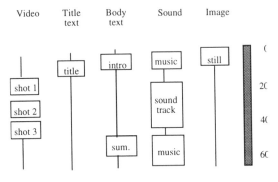

Figure 1.13: *CMIFed Parallel View.* Time flows from top to bottom as indicated in the time line at the far right. Columns represent the different channels used by the presentation, and boxes in each column represent events assigned to that channel. The placement and size of a box are indications of the start and duration of the event.

1.3.2   Radiological Hypermedia

Hypermedia has many applications in the health care domain. The goal of a hypermedia archiving and communication system for radiologists is to provide various kinds of *medical data* in such a way that they can be quickly retrieved and reviewed by authorized personnel [43]. A referring clinician often needs to arrange a meeting with a particular radiologist to discuss a patient because this hardly can be done over the phone, as images and other data are involved. There is an incentive to (partially) replace such contacts through hypermedia.

The *RAdiological REporting using MultiMedia ANnotations* (RAREMMAN) system is a report creation and presentation system. RAREMMAN offers the reporting radiologist an image window to view the diagnostic images needed and a text window to enter the text of his report. The text window is implemented by a program that has been extended to allow the entrance of active labels (see Figure 1.14). When such a label is entered in the text, RAREMMAN gives the radiologist the opportunity to choose an image and to put an annotation at a spatial position in the image. Active labels realize a mapping from positions in the report to positions in an image. The report that has been edited in this way can be saved and sent to the corresponding clinician. The clinician can also annotate the report by voice (see Figure 1.15). The possibility to employ active annotations is well appreciated by user groups [25].

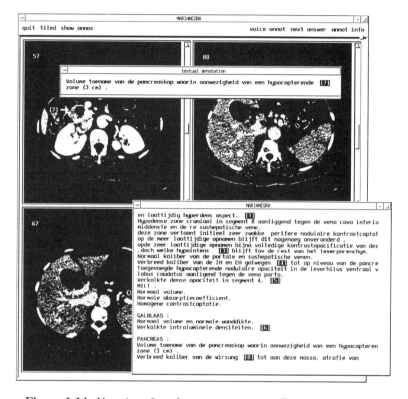

Figure 1.14: *User interface for report creation.* Examples of active labels are shown in the text window as black-on-white [x] character strings, where x is a numeral. An annotation is composed of an arrow and the [x] label. The appearance of such annotations can be changed by the user (as shown in the upper right corner). The radiologist can add text and labels.

1.4 Networks and the World Wide Web

Since the 1990s the popularity of large computers serving many users has given way to the situation in which many small machines connected via a network share resources. The kinds of sharing, the ways of communicating, and the applications of these *networks* are all vital to the modern organization. For machines in a network to communicate many conventions must be established and followed. New and vast libraries of material are available via network. One of the most heavily used network

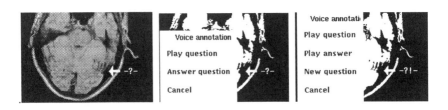

Figure 1.15: *Handling voice annotations.* Images from the RAREMMAN screen which illustrate the handling of voice annotations. As shown on the left of the figure a question annotation -?- can be put at a certain position in the image and the clinician can speak in a question. The radiologist now receives the document with the voice annotations displayed. He can activate these annotations as shown in the middle of the figure. By clicking on the arrow, a menu pops up to listen to the question or to answer it. When the question is answered the annotation changes to ?!

systems uses the Internet Protocol and is called the *Internet*. Many non-Internet networks have provided connections to the Internet so that it has become indirectly a connector of the world's networks. The World Wide Web supports browsing on the Internet [53].

1.4.1 Terminology

A computer network is a set of computers communicating by common conventions, called protocols, over communication media [102]. Each computer of any size in the network is called either a machine or a system, although the term system is sometimes used to denote the entire network. The machines in a network are called network nodes. Machines that users directly access are called hosts. *Hosts* have their own resources such as disks, user mailboxes, and user accounts. The building where a group of nodes is located is called a site. *Protocols* are used to manage the exchange of information in the network over the physical medium, such as wires or radio waves. Information is exchanged in discrete units called messages. Because of size limitations of either the physical medium or the protocol, messages are fragmented into packets. Packets may be routed into different networks and be reassembled into the original message when they reach their destination node. Computer networks may be combined and connected to form larger networks of networks. A host used to connect the networks may be referred to as a gateway.

The resources which networks might share include software packages and information storage facilities. This sharing may conform to the *client/server model* in which the machine containing the resource (the server) responds to requests from the other machines (the clients). In contrast, in a distributed model each machine contains some of the resource and the computers communicate on equal terms. In either case, coordination is critical.

One spectrum along which computer networks are described corresponds to their geographical dispersion. *Local area networks* (LANs) consist of collections of computers in a single building managed by one organization. In contrast, a *wide area network* (WAN) links machines that are widely separated, be it across a city or the world. The Internet is an example of a world-wide network. LANs are likely to be produced and serviced by one company. WANs are usually open in the sense that many different hardware and software systems from different companies can communicate effectively with a WAN.

1.4.2   Internet

The term Internet originates from the protocol on which the Internet depends, namely the *Internet Protocol* (IP). The basic mechanism of the network is that one computer sends a message to another computer. To send a message on the network, a computer puts its data in an envelope, the IP packet, and addresses the packet to the target computer.

In the United States in 1969 the Advanced Research Projects Agency (ARPA) demonstrated the viability of a IP computer network called *ARPAnet*. The original motivation for development was resource sharing, as ARPA noticed many contractors were tending to request the same resources. The network was designed to be tolerant of failure of nodes within the network. Each computer can talk to each other computer in the network as a peer and must assume some responsibility for the integrity of the messages it sends and receives.

Researchers almost immediately began using the ARPAnet for collaboration through electronic mail and other services. The high utility of the network led people to want *increased connectivity*. By the early 1980s, local area networks of Unix workstations began to be popular. These systems typically included IP networking capability. Many organizations in which these networks were placed wanted to connect the ARPANet to their local network so that each user of the local area network would also through that network have access to the ARPANet.

In the late 1980s one could say that the Internet was all the networks using the IP protocol that cooperate to form a seamless network for their collective users [73]. However, other networks, such as *Bitnet* and *DECNet,* have translators that take Internet messages and send them to Bitnet or DECNet addresses and conversely. These translators sit on computers called gateways and the Internet in a sense extends over these gateways across a wider set of computers than those literally using the IP protocols.

The Internet has a strong 'grass roots' character. The ultimate authority for the direction of the Internet rests with the *Internet Society.* The Internet Society is a voluntary membership organization whose purpose is to promote global information exchange through Internet technology. The Society appoints a group of volunteers to approve new Internet standards, to develop rules about the assignment of addresses, and to take other management-like positions. This group is called the Internet Architecture Board and is again composed of volunteers. The Internet is not owned by any one company. Instead *everyone owns* and pays for their own part.

Internet growth has been phenomenal. In January, 1993 about 1,300,000 different sites were hosts on the Internet and in January, 1994 that number had risen to 2,220,000, an impressive 70% increase [44]. By May, 1994 the Internet included over 31,000 networks with one network being added every 10 minutes; the number of computers connected through the Internet exceeded two million; and over 20 million people had access to Internet resources [76]. Although the Internet was originally developed for research-related purposes, by May, 1994 commercial users had exceeded 50% of the connected base and commercial usage was growing most rapidly.

1.4.3   World Wide Web

The *World Wide Web* (WWW) was developed to be a pool of human knowledge that people across time and space could share. The WWW began at the European Particle Physics Laboratory (called CERN) in Geneva, Switzerland. There scientists collaborate with many other scientists around the world on the subject of high energy physics. A small collaborative hypertext system was developed at CERN to facilitate electronic collaboration. This initial Web was designed so that if used independently for two projects across which connections were later discovered, then these connections could easily be added to the Web information space without having to rewrite the information [9]. This property of the Web has facilitated its connection to other sources of information on the Internet and ultimately to a world-wide information space.

Three key features of the WWW are:

- the address system,
- a network protocol, and
- a hypertext markup language.

These three features are extensions of the *Internet* and fully compatible with it. They allow properly structured Internet information to have a new kind of accessibility.

The address system is based on *Universal Resource Identifiers* (URIs). URIs are strings which address objects on the WWW. URIs are universal in that they encode members of the universal set of network addresses. The URI syntax reserves the '/' as a way of representing hierarchical space. Relative names exploit the hierarchical structure and allow links to be made independent of the higher parts of the URI, such as the server name.

The *HyperText Transfer Protocol* (HTTP) is a protocol for transferring information efficiently and for retrieving documents in an unbounded and extensible set of formats. The client sends a weighted list of the formats it can handle, and the server replies with the data in any of those formats.

With the *Hypertext Markup Language* (HTML), authors can define links from one location in a file to other locations in the same file or to other files on the Internet. HTML includes simple structure elements, such as several levels of headings and bulleted lists. A WWW viewer translates HTML statements into various screen presentations.

The first WWW access programs were written at CERN. Subsequently, the National Center for Supercomputer Applications at the University of Illinois made available a viewer called *Mosaic* which became very popular. Many viewers or browsers are now freely available.

A user typically begins a trip in the WWW from a *home page* of her own institution (see Figure 1.16). This home page should also provide routes to the rest of the WWW. One of the big attractions of the WWW is the ease with which graphics and, more generally, *multimedia* are available. In addition to the hypertext links that readily take one from one section of text to another, a WWW document readily links to sounds, videos, or animations (see Figure 1.17).

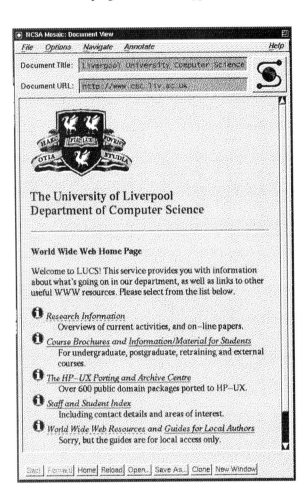

Figure 1.16: *Local WWW Home Page*: An example of accessing the WWW from the University of Liverpool with the Mosaic viewer.

1.5   Education

The use of *courseware* can be described as 'teaching through computers' [116] and refers to the presentation of lesson material and questions on the material, through a computer, providing student interaction and feedback. Courseware packages are tools that can be used to present materials in novel ways, not easily available through other media, and with the flexibility to adapt to different learning and teaching styles.   This is useful because different students think and learn in different ways depending on the subject matter of the course and the experience of the student.

1.5.1 Instruction Cycle

The 'Instructional Cycle' characteristic of Western educational systems represents the development and delivery of lessons at any grade level or subject matter (see Figure 1.18). In the traditional lifecycle a single teacher is usually in charge of the development and delivery of the lesson. Courseware development corresponds to the preparation phase in the Instruction Cycle [127].

Behaviorist models form the basis for realization of many computer-assisted instruction products. The behavioristic approach to CAI is characterized by educational objectives that are stated in terms of performance. The performance is composed of actions that can be observed, verified, and controlled by quantitative methods and which the student is able to perform after having completed the specific educational path.

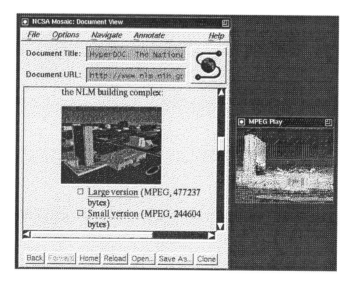

Figure 1.17: *WWW Video:* From the home page in the previous figure, the user has traversed to other WWW server directories and from there to the American National Library of Medicine (NLM). The WWW information about the NLM includes an animated tour of the facilities which is encoded in MPEG. The left window shows the Mosaic interface with the option to choose the small or large version of the MPEG animation. The small window on the right is actually running the animated view of the NLM.

One behavioristic *taxonomy* proposes six different types of intellectual abilities [12]:

Knowledge Capacity to remember or to recognize specific and general elements.
Comprehension Capacity to utilize knowledge possessed, using three types of operations.
Application Capacity to utilize in concrete situations, principles, laws, and rules, previously acquired.
Analysis Capacity to recognize and isolate the elements that make up a whole and the capacity to establish the principles which regulate the relationship between such elements.
Synthesis Capacity to collect and collate a series of isolated elements in such a way that a well-organized and coherent whole will result.
Evaluation Capacity to express judgments on the contents or on the methods used to reach a conclusion.

The most used technique, to passage from instrument to performance, is based on establishing a connection between taxonomy and *observed behavior*, by means of action verbs. Such a technique is characterized by the fact that the objectives are defined in terms of expected results, as the final behaviors of the student at the end of the specific course unit. The final behavior will lead to the use of the capacities categorized in the taxonomy, which will be recognized in practice in the action verb used. In short, every educational objective must answer three questions:

- What will the student be able to do?
- What tools will he have at his disposal?
- With what degree of accuracy?

Learning is the change induced by education in the behavior of the student.

1.5.2   Lesson Design

Courseware authoring systems are for the development of courseware. In many cases they include authoring languages that include some of the structural features of programming languages but focus on supporting common instructional functions, like asking multiple-choice questions and assessing the response [7][70]. Authoring systems provide a method for individuals with little or no programming or even design expertise to create lessons [81].

A *frame* may be defined as the contents of any single screen of information [17]. Lessons that vary the location of information within frames can be frustrating. The adoption of consistent, standardized conventions for frame design is often necessary [46] [60].

One classification of lesson types covers tutorials, drill and practice, and simulations. *Tutorials* model the best techniques available for tutoring students. *Drill and practice* has the objective of reinforcing existing knowledge. Practice, feedback, and remediation are partners in a continuous teaching cycle. Simulations approximate, replicate, or emulate the features of some task, setting, or context. *Simulations* are used when the costs of alternative teaching systems are prohibitively high, when it is impossible to study the concepts of interest in 'real-time', or when the risks are considered sufficiently high to require demonstration of competence in a controlled, relatively risk-free environment [1].

Another classification of lesson types is related to the evolving characteristics of authoring tools:

Branching   In the 1960s computer-assisted instruction was marked by two major events. The first was the birth of 'branching programs' based on the assumption that the learner's response could be used to control the material to be shown next to him/her. This was also accompanied by the birth of 'author languages' specially designed for teaching materials.

Generative   In the 1970s, with 'generative' systems, it was possible — in some domains such as arithmetic and grammar — to give general teaching strategies, and the system to produce a tree of possible interactions.

Intelligent   Since the 1980s research in the areas of cognitive science, knowledge representation, cognitive psychology, artificial intelligence, and didactics have led to Intelligent Tutoring Systems that are able to represent and manage the knowledge of the task domain, the history of the learner's behavior, and the set of possible teaching strategies.

The lesson design activity is a very creative task and involves different kinds of skills. One method for idea generation for building lessons is known as *brainstorming* [1]. During this process, people involved in courseware design produce as many ideas as possible; emphasizing quantitative aspects rather than qualitative ones and postponing decisions concerning quality and relevance. Some ideas, produced during the brainstorming activity, will be eliminated later according to basic principles regarding, for instance, subject matter and instructional strategies. The remaining ideas must be analyzed to define a suitable teaching sequence. Many ways exist to analyze these ideas, but two methods are often used: task and concept analysis.

Task analysis has been used for designing instructional models. This approach helps in breaking down complex skills into more elementary skills obtaining a hierarchy of the learner's skills and behaviors. It is possible to obtain a task analysis tree that describes the subdivision of skills where the terminal level corresponds to the entry-level skills of the student. From another perspective task analysis produces a flowchart illustrating what someone must do to perform a given activity[130].

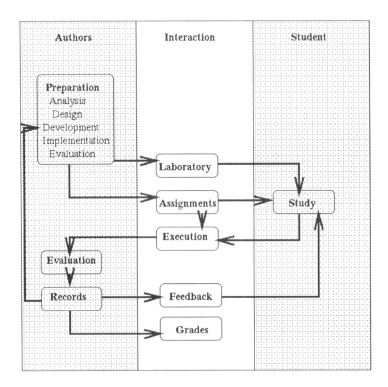

Figure 1.18: *The Instructional Cycle.* The nine phases fall into three categories in terms of the authority that functions within each phase. Three of the phases, namely 'Preparation', 'Evaluation', and 'Record keeping' require teacher involvement only. On the other hand, the 'Study' phase requires student activities only. The remaining phases of 'Class/Lab', 'Assignments', 'Execution', 'Feedback', and 'Grades' provides a common information space where both teacher and students interact.

Concept analysis may be used to analyze skills and subject matter. The subject matter is organized in concepts and their relationships. A concept is defined as a group of objects, events, or relationships sharing a set of common features and therefore representing a class. The common and essential characteristics of concept members are called relevant features. The other features may be classified either as incidental features or irrelevant features. This approach is generally useful in producing a teaching sequence that starts with the relevant features.

Different approaches have been used in structuring curricula [147]. One of these approaches is known as *Learner-Oriented Knowledge Representation.* In this approach, the curriculum is split into three conceptual layers. At the top are central issues of expertise, called techniques. The techniques are composed of lower level knowledge units called skills and organized as networks. Finally, skills are related to the various tasks that involve them (see Figure 1.19).

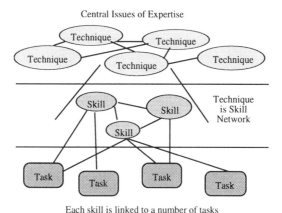

Figure 1.19: *Basic Instructional Program System.* The three conceptual layers are formed as ordered networks. A technique comprises a number of skills, each of which is made up of a number of tasks.

The learner-oriented knowledge model represents elementary skills as nodes connected by relations, such as generalization or analogy. Although this organization is focused on representation of *conceptual relations* among the nodes of the graph, other approaches include explicit connection to a hierarchy of curricular goals. This kind of architecture organizes the system around pedagogical issues. Each issue is a miniature system focused on a specific piece of the subject matter, and includes knowledge about its conceptual relations to other issues, such as part/whole or analogical relations, and knowledge about its curricular relations to other issues, such as pre- and postrequisites so that it can trigger remedial actions. This approach allows a variety of instructional strategies to be adopted with minimal modification of the knowledge base. The modularity of this scheme allows flexibility in reusing portions of a system for other domains.

1.5.3   Courseware Examples

A large amount of *courseware* has been developed over the years. In this section two examples are provided from the medical domain. This is not to suggest that medicine is the prime example of a domain for courseware application. Many disciplines are using courseware (see Figure 1.20).

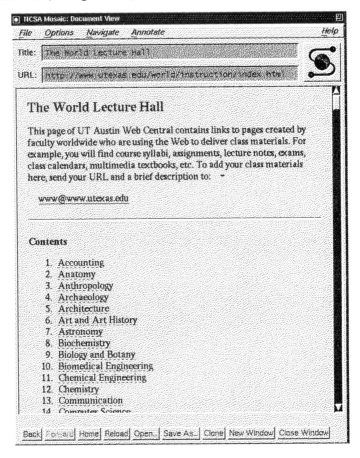

Figure 1.20: *Catalogue of Courseware*: This window on the www.ut.edu home page shows the beginning of the long list of topics for which pointers to courseware is maintained.

In 1985, the Cornell School of Medicine began experimenting with the idea of using computers to make the learning process more efficient [32]. As a result, students taking the course Introductory Pathology can enroll in an electronic version PathMac of the course. Macintosh computers tied into the PathMac database are scattered throughout the campus for student access. Students can study online textbooks, run simulated laboratories, or test their mastery of physiology by viewing online dissections.

PathMac provides online access to approximately seven gigabytes of images and bibliographical material that can be searched intelligently, cross-referenced, and printed. Software includes applications written in HyperCard, Guide, and other software tools developed in-house. The opening screen allows students to indicate which course they are taking. A selection of materials is available for biochemistry, anatomy, neuroscience, parasitology, physiology, radiology, and pathology.

At the Ancona Medical School in Italy computer lessons have been written on rheumatoid arthritis and lymphoadenopathies following the hypertext architecture of the program Guide. This architecture provides for the multilevelled organization of information using 'notes', 'buttons', and 'cross-references'. Key sentences cross-reference points to the next page in a lesson; or expand to obtain further details. Interactive, high-definition black-and-white and color images are included to help the student, particularly to illustrate medical procedures with radiological images.

One Ancona Medical School courseware *simulation* deals with a young man who presented with a severe asthmatic attack after a walk (see Figure 1.21). The season is spring and the walk was in the countryside, both facts suggesting an allergic etiology of the disease. If the student's choice is to perform the case history or the skin tests, the computerized tutor comments that the choice is wrong given that the priority is to relieve the patient's symptoms. An essential physical examination and appropriate treatment should be immediately performed. Once the prescription of the correct medication results in normalization of the respiratory sound and congratulations from the tutor, a case history may be taken. The tutor emphasizes the key questions that should be asked in order to determine the possible allergic origin of a respiratory disease. The student performs the skin tests and evaluates the reactions. Diagnosis of the allergy pollens may be made and a correct hyposensitizing treatment planned.

The experiences with courseware at the Ancona Medical School were positive. It was concluded that courseware provided an effective learning environment that could be used to *supplement,* but not replace, traditional methods. The direct management of a patient in distress evoked sympathy on the part of the student, which indicated that the hypermedia could provide a link between theory and bedside practice.

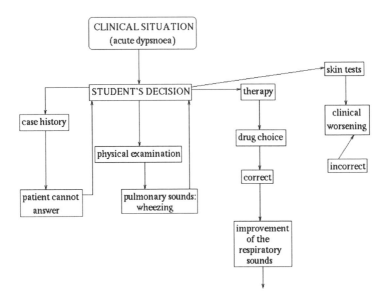

Figure 1.21: *Flow chart.* Flow chart describing all routes that the student may follow managing the simulated patients affected by allergic asthma [27].

1.5.4   Benefits

Technology-supported teaching can [125]:

* support *interactive learning* and
* free the teacher from *repetitive tasks.*

In well-designed drill and practice courseware, students can receive quick and accurate feedback, and progress at flexible rates, without public approbation of their errors. Information technology may now be used in education, as books, audio-visual equipment, the blackboard and, indeed, the teacher have been used for many years.

There is a Chinese proverb that states:

I hear, I forget,
I see, I remember,

I do, I understand.

The effect of *doing* profoundly affects the ability of the student to understand what is being taught. Gathering information comes about through activity and students must be motivated in order to learn effectively. Students can use the computer to perform practical tasks and their motivation is upheld through the combination of 'seeing', 'hearing', and 'doing', which are features of a number of courseware packages.

There are a number of advantages of computer-based instruction which are viewed in terms of cost reduction and improvement of effectiveness. Those predominantly *reducing cost* are:

- Reduced training time.
- Reduced reliance on trained instructors.
- Reduced need for use of expensive or possibly dangerous operational equipment.

Those predominantly *increasing effectiveness* are:

- Provide consistent, high quality instruction available on a large scale.
- Provide hands-on, performance-oriented instruction.
- Permit individualization of instruction.

The application of computer-based instruction is one way of increasing the cost effectiveness of education. Uniformly high quality instruction is possible with computers as they eliminate variability caused by differences between instructors. With this technology, a long-term goal of educators can be realized by distributing instruction to students rather than by distributing students to instruction [94]. With capabilities of centrally updating instructional materials, many logistical problems can be avoided, and electronic transfer of information may be cheaper than paper transmission of information. Furthermore, student time to learn a subject may be reduced with computer-based instruction [96].

1.6   Conclusion

Hypertext provides conceptual links among blocks of text. Multimedia is synchronized media, such as a voice with moving image. *Hypermedia* is the combination of the two namely, synchronized media that additionally have conceptual links between their components. For instance, the presentation of a hypermedia video might allow the user to point to an object in the video and to then see an additional window appear on the screen in which descriptive text about the object appears.

The *Dexter model* of hypertext is based on nodes and links. This model can be extended to account for timing. Individual nodes are then associated with several media that will start and stop at prescribed times relative to one another. Thus one has both conceptual linking and time-based synchronization in this extended Dexter model.

In the Introduction to this chapter the *World Wide Web* was introduced, and the question was asked 'is the World Wide Web hypertext, multimedia, or hypermedia?' Links are vital to the World Wide Web, and its popularity is based in part on its ease of handling images, sound, and video. The World Wide Web does not, however, offer timing options to the author or reader. Nevertheless, as it offers hypertext features along with multiple media, in common parlance it might conveniently be considered a kind of hypermedia.

Hypermedia appeals to the senses of people, but has such vast storage and computing requirements that its diffusion in the world is tightly connected to the advance of technology [142]. The direction of the *market* depends in part on the match between available hypermedia, such as digitized radiological videos with voice annotations, and available hypermedia systems, such as the Multimedia Personal Computer [112].

In an ambitious aim for *classroom computers,* teachers abandon the worksheet curriculum and confidently allow students' minds to develop through the exploration of computer simulated worlds [97]. This statement may seen extreme, but there is a widely held view that hypermedia is providing the means for a new type of education. The belief that computers could support learning has been shared by influential people for decades[139], but new, affordable hypermedia systems are helping this belief become a reality.

2
Coordination

Numerous guides or cookbooks exist for authors of educational hypermedia. Often these guides focus on the development of ideas into pedagogically useful presentations [145]. Astute courseware developers have also, however, long recognized the importance of teamwork or *coordination*.

2.1   The Need

Some lecturers develop course materials in isolation. Such a practice might hamper the development of courseware, as a production team approach may be the best method to develop courseware [100]. To better understand the situation a *survey* was conducted among academics at the *University of Liverpool*. A questionnaire was sent to 90 members of academic staff at the University of Liverpool, randomly chosen from a list of staff in all departments of the University. Questions asked respondents to rank their answers on a prescribed scale and there was also an opportunity to add comments. The following analysis is based on the answers [79].

Responses obtained indicate that teachers see *collaboration* as being an important aspect of course development. As expected, almost all respondents (over 90%) say that collaboration takes place at department level, with colleagues who are known and communication is not problematic. Other departments are also important when developing strategies (nearly 80% agree) but are less important as sources of specific material. Although respondents seem enthusiastic about collaboration, they appear less enthusiastic about taking material developed elsewhere and using it. This may be a contributing factor to the slow uptake of courseware. Lecturers feel that technical support is required when adapting a hypermedia educational package to their requirements, and this may be difficult to obtain, if the material has been developed outside their institution.

Academics often feel that they do not have the technical skills and *computer expertise* necessary to develop and implement effective educational hypermedia. Some staff think that the traditional methods they employ at the moment, for example lectures, will have to change and they want help in doing this. Most also want hardware provision dedicated to each department and technical support, both department-based and throughout the University. This may again reflect the lack of confidence many feel in using computers in a teaching context. A procedure for quality assurance is also desired by some, indicating a desire to get standards set from the beginning. Linked to this is the idea of a courseware library (91% think this is either very important or moderately important), which could be used to store examples of good courseware and possibly allow its reuse. Procedures to coordinate people are seen as being necessary by many, supporting the previous findings that collaboration is a key issue in courseware development.

To provide a more complete picture, responses were examined according to whether the respondents had:

• experience of using courseware or
• no experience of using courseware.

Collaboration is an important issue for both groups. All nonuser respondents see collaboration within the department as being vital, but a quarter of the courseware users are unsure of its merits. This is possibly because the *courseware users* often forced to work in isolation when developing courseware and so are more used to working independently, or it may be because they seldom find colleagues in their own departments with whom to work. Most of those in both groups feel that it is beneficial to look for specific ideas from elsewhere.

Several questionnaire respondents suggested that a *courseware center* should be set up with the remit to provide support for courseware developers. This may be a somewhat ambitious plan in the present economic climate, but an initial starting block would be the forming of a Courseware Development Group. The Group should provide some staff training and workshops to improve confidence in nontechnical minded teachers. Through this Group the support infrastructure for courseware could be built up, with frequent feedback from those it is designed to help.

The development and deployment of educational hypermedia is occurring on larger and larger scales. For example, the Maricopa Community Colleges in Arizona are some of the largest community colleges in the world and have invested heavily in college-wide development and use of educational hypermedia (see Figure 2.1). This kind of effort requires excellent coordination among the people who are using the technology.

2.2   Coordination Theory

Coordination may be defined as the act of working together harmoniously and *coordination theory* is the body of principles describing how this should be achieved with respect to how [78]:

- activities can be coordinated or
- actors can work together harmoniously.

There must be one or more actors, performing some activities that are directed towards some ends or goals. The goal-relevant relationships between the activities are interdependencies.

If there is no interdependence, there is nothing to coordinate. *Interdependence* between activities can be analyzed in terms of common objects that constrain how each activity is performed. For example, a course can not be properly designed until the objectives of the course have been defined. This pattern of interdependence is called a prerequisite, and other patterns include 'shared resource' and 'simultaneity'. One way in which technology can help manage these interdependencies is simply by helping to detect them in the first place.

Coordination may be described in terms of successively deeper levels of underlying processes. For instance, many coordination processes require that some *decision* has been made and accepted by a group. Group decisions, in turn, require members of the group to communicate in some form. This *communication* requires that some messages be transported in a language that is understandable to both. Finally, the establishment of this language depends on the ability of actors to perceive common objects. The strongest dependencies are downward through these layers (see Figure 2.2).

2.3 Group Processes and Roles

A *collaborative activity* is a process that can be characterized along three fundamental dimensions: temporal, spatial, and interactive. *Temporal characteristics* reflect the nature of concurrency and order of cooperative work in a group. *Spatial characteristics* include the size and proximity of a group, and *interactive characteristics* represent dynamic mechanisms in response to the changing environmental and individual factors.

Group development follows a reasonably consistent pattern that involves a period of orientation, resolution of conflicts about authority and personal relations, and a productive period. An investigation into the character of group work has produced a model which shows that collaboration progresses from initiation to execution to presentation. Although the computer can support each of these three stages, direct person-to-person contact is important, particularly in the initiation stage.

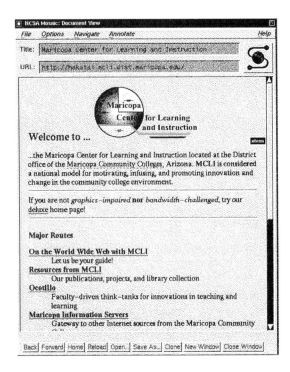

Figure 2.1: *Maricopa Colleges:* This window from http://hakati.mcli.dist.maricopa.edu shows the introduction to the Maricopa Center for Learning and Instruction. This Center helps coordinate the development and use of educational hypermedia across an enormous community college population.

Communication patterns and the quality of group interaction are partly determined by seating arrangement. Persons with the greatest visual centrality speak most often. Indeed it is from this *centralized group* that a leader is most likely to arise. A decentralized communication network is most efficient when the group must solve complex problems, whereas a centralized network is most efficient when the group must solve simple problems.

To a large extent, the behavior patterns of a group depend on group size [21]. As membership increases, the number of potential information exchanges rises geometrically, and the frequency, duration, and intimacy of information exchange all decline. Consensus becomes harder to achieve, and affectional ties and satisfaction with the group all decline with the possibility of fractional smaller subgroups being formed [62]. There is greater interest in giving information and less interest in asking opinion, giving opinion or showing agreement.

Process Level	Components	Examples of Generic Processes
Coordination	goals, activities, actors	identifying goals, ordering activities, assigning activities to actors, allocating resources, synchronizing activities
Group decision making	goals, actors, alternatives, evaluations, choices	proposing alternatives, evaluating alternatives, making choices (e.g. by authority consensus or voting)
Communication	senders, receivers, messages, languages	establishing common languages, selecting receiver (routing), transporting message (delivering)
Perception of common objects	actors, objects	seeming same physical objects, accessing shared database

Figure 2.2: *Processes Underlying Coordination.* Levels of Coordination and correspondent representations are identified, particularly in terms of generic processes.

In one model of work (see Figure 2.3), people are assigned certain *roles* and they work in parallel. Role definition and assignment is done according to people's expertise. Each person contributes one or more specialties to the work. A manager coordinates the collaboration. Each person has a strong sense of involvement. The identification of a number of different roles does not imply that each role is filled by a different person, but a person could be charged with more than one role or a role could be filled by more than one person. It is important to assign precise roles to people, because without a clear definition and sharing of responsibilities, at a given moment some team members could be repeating other people's work. If roles are not filled by people with appropriate skills, the product will suffer.

General roles that people usually play in a working intellectual team include Innovator, Resource Investigator, Chair, Shaper, Evaluator, Team Worker, Organizer, and Finisher. Each role has special characteristics and is necessary to team success, these are the [101]:

1. *Innovator* thinks up new ideas.
2. *Resource Investigator* brings information and ideas to the group, but from sources outside the group.
3. *Chair* is the social leader of the group whose skills lie in spotting what each member does best and in guiding the group towards success.

4.   *Shaper* provides the energy and drive to implement ideas and get work moving.
5.   *Evaluator* critically appraises proposals, monitors progress, and prevents the group making mistakes.
6.   *Team Worker* provides an informal network of communication and support which continues outside meetings.
7.   *Organizer* translates plans into manageable tasks.
8.   *Finisher* worries about what can go wrong, and maintains a permanent sense of urgency which communicates itself to the group.

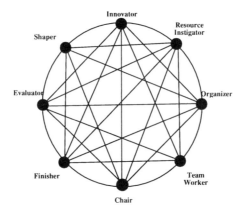

Figure 2.3: *Work Model.* The key team members interact with all the other team members.

2.4   Coordinated Group Communications

Modeling working groups and organizations is expected to help predict behavior in the workplace and thus enable the building of tools that would enhance work. This section looks at one particular tool for modeling organizations. Courseware development will in a later chapter be described through the *modeling language.*

The *Activity Model Environment* (AME) is an object-oriented tool for exploring models of organizations [134]. The AME tool consists of a database and an associated rule-based formalism for representing activities and organizational states. Users interact with the model by creating and playing roles. Activity related communication proceeds via the exchange of messages between roles. Eight components of the framework can be identified:

- *Activities* are sets of tasks for achieving a goal.
- *People* are placeholders for actual individuals.
- *Roles* specify the responsibilities and duties of people.
- *Workspaces* contain resources associated with roles.
- *Messages* are objects that flow between the role instances associated with an activity.
- *Information Units* are used in building messages.
- *Rules* constrain the behavior of components.
- *Functions* are performed by roles and messages as part of an activity.

In AME, roles, people, workspaces, units and *messages* are represented as objects and are stored in the *Organizational Manual,* which is a database acting as reference both for users of the AME and for the AME itself. Activities are sets of tasks that are performed by groups of role instances to achieve a set goal. The description of an activity provides input/output states as well as roles and *messages* involved in its execution.

People have object entries in the *Organizational Manual* associated with them. Each entry specifies the roles that each person is authorized to play. A person interacts with AME through specified role instances. Each person may hold several role instances at any one time. Roles define responsibilities that are taken by one or more people. A role instance consists of the person instance undertaking the role, the set of role rules, and a role agent. The role agent is executed by the system and might undertake some of the person's responsibilities. The role agent uses the role rules in the performance of the role.

A workspace is a conceptual work area that contains resources associated with a particular role. Multiple role instances may be associated with a workspace. The workspace also contains message handling resources. *Messages* are used for role instances communication. *Messages* collect and transfer information associated with activities between roles. They exist for the lifetime of an activity. There are different types of *messages* (e.g. memos, notices, forms). *Messages* are composed of groups of information units, which are atomic information objects. An unit has a name, fields, and a set of completion rules associated with it.

Rules define and constrain the behavior of roles, messages, and units under specified conditions. *Functions* are atomic operations performed within group communication (e.g. instantiate-message, fill-field). They must be executed entirely by one role instance or role agent.

2.5   Computer Mediated Communication

Although *electronic communication* in some ways allows separated group members to interact as if they are in close physical proximity, there are some distinct differences in exchange activities of remote and face-to-face groups [132]. Groups using computer-mediated communication, when compared with face-to-face groups, participate more equally within the group, are more uninhibited, and reach decisions that deviate further from initial individual preferences. However, interpersonal conflict tends to be greater, communication becomes less efficient, and satisfaction with the group process tends to decline.

From the technology point of view, the basic components of a computer-based communication system include [61]:

- terminal,
- phone line,
- a computer system that provides the hardware and software for handling the communication and also a centralized storage of the communication transcripts,
- a digital data network for low-cost digital-data transmission.

Many *networks* now exist with different organizational and technological characteristics. These different networks increase interconnectivity at the organizational level and are advancing rapidly in terms of their technological speed and capacity.

There are two kinds of services that computer networks provide to users:

- resource sharing and
- computer-mediated communication.

Resource sharing allows users to access and use resources on another computer that they cannot directly (in physical terms) access. The services provided include remote login, file transfer. Computer-mediated communication allows users to exchange messages either synchronously or in an asynchronous fashion. Systems include computer conferencing, bulletin boards, telephony, electronic mail, and video conferencing systems [102].

2.6   Groupware

Software to support groups is called groupware. In the early 1960s Engelbart created a laboratory at Stanford Research Institute to explore the use of computers to augment group work [36]. In 1981 Trudy Johnson-Lenz and Peter Johnson-Lenz introduced the term groupware to mean:

> intentional group processes and procedures to achieve specific purposes, plus software tools designed to support and facilitate the group's work [69].

This definition of groupware emphasizes the union of group activities and its software support. Groupware is effective when it is designed to match the group needs.

Computer-Supported Collaborative Work (CSCW) is an interdisciplinary field that focuses on exploiting groupware to augment team work. The term CSCW was coined in 1984 [5]. When the term CSCW was coined it simply designated multiple people working together and using computers to support and augment their work. It was soon realized that designing such systems requires a thorough understanding of the nature of cooperative work [6][121][124].

CSCW may be seen as a conjunction of certain kinds of technologies, certain kinds of users (often small, self-directed professional teams) and a worldview that emphasizes convivial work relations. These three elements taken together differentiate CSCW from other related forms of computerization, such as information systems and office automation [72]. CSCW and groupware refer to the same body of scientific and engineering work. Two main streams characterize research efforts within this domain. Computer scientists and electrical engineers form the first stream that led to development of such applications as decision support systems, collaborative writing systems, and coordination tools. The second stream is formed by academics in such disciplines as sociology, psychology, and education who investigate how the people employ the technology.

Companies from a wide range of fields are interested in CSCW and groupware. Vendor companies are interested because they foresee a new market for products that support small groups [49]. Telecommunication and network companies are interested because they realize the need for connectivity, concurrent processing, and high bandwidth. In general, companies are interested because they want to use technology to support teams and projects [150].

GroupSystems is an electronic meeting support system that was developed at the University of Arizona. It was installed at more than 22 universities and 12 companies and has been used by more than 30,000 people. Although GroupSystems is designed to support a variety of tasks by different groups, a common pattern of use emerged through its use in universities and corporations (see Figure 2.4).

The *GroupSystems architecture* consist of three major components a meeting room, a meeting facilitator, and a software toolkit [91]. The minimum configuration includes a network of color graphics microcomputer workstations equipped with hard disks available to meeting group members. An additional one or two workstations constitute the facilitator's console. A large-screen video display, connected with the workstations, is provided along with additional audio-visual equipment (e.g. overhead projectors).

The chairman of the meeting is called the *meeting facilitator*. The facilitator may be the group leader, a group member, or another person neutral and separate from the group. The meeting facilitator provides the technical support needed to use the software tools and thus reduces the need for training for novice users. The meeting facilitator also assumes the responsibility of chairing the meeting, maintaining the agenda, and structuring and maintaining group knowledge and memory.

Usually the leader of the group wishing to use the system meets the GroupSystems facilitator and develops the meeting's agenda. The meeting starts with a *brainstorming phase*. Participants type in their ideas or comments in the workstation and the system collects and displays the data on large screens in front of the participants as well as in their workstation displays. At the end of this phase the ideas are organized into a set of key ideas followed by a prioritization process which results in a short list of ideas. Then the participants make plans of how to realize the ideas. The process is repeated until consensus is reached.

Although GroupSystems support meetings, *GroupWrite* [41] supports collaboration between authors that are widely distributed and do not have access to communication networks. Collaborators communicate by exchanging word processor files that contain draft versions of the main document and a history of the changes in the main document. In GroupWrite, existing and familiar word processing functionality has been simply augmented by version control facilities that support group writing.

GroupWrite supports *version management* at two levels of document detail: (a) entire document and (b) paragraph level. Different versions are linked together as well as the paragraphs within a version. Cross-links between paragraphs in different versions are also maintained. The users are able to create such links while the system maintains them and notifies users, who access a version of a document, of the existing links.

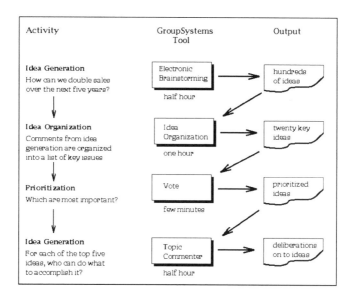

Figure 2.4: *GroupSystems pattern of use.* The activities of the group are depicted on the far left; the relevant tool, in the middle; and the output, on the far right [91].

Managing versions at the above two levels (document and paragraph) allow the reuse not only of the entire document but also of the parts of it.

The *user interface* has been designed to meet the needs of users with varying levels of expertise. A novice may use the system as a conventional word processor. A more advanced user may view it as a word processor with versioning facilities. Expert users may view it as a hypertext system. The user interface is also similar to the ones of widely available word processors with which users are familiar.

Although GroupWrite supports asynchronous communication, other tools support synchronous communication. For instance, SharedARK (Shared Alternate Reality Kit) is a distributed multimedia environment that provides to an arbitrary number of users a *shared workspace*. The users can interact in real time with the same real-world physical objects. The system is equipped with a hands-free hi-fi audio link as well as a video link (see Figure 2.5). The video link consists of a camera and a monitor that enables users to establish eye contact.

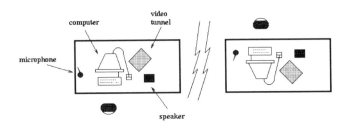

Figure 2.5: *SharedARK setting.* Each user has a desktop computer, a video tunnel, and audio equipment.

2.7   Collaborative Learning

In traditional higher educational environments students principally learn by attending lectures and taking notes. Secondary to this is the undertaking of assignments and performing of experiments to emphasize the instruction they have received. Using collaborative hypermedia a group of students may collectively be involved in the development of a piece of work. This could mean that a better piece of work is produced as the opinions, thoughts, and ideas of many (as opposed to one) are amalgamated and refined. Results indicate that grouping does not reduce but frequently improves achievement and attitudes when learning [29]. Communication of ideas, views, and knowledge is central to the educational process, and technology may influence this process for both student-teacher and student-student interaction [71].

Intermedia is the networked hypermedia system developed at Brown University. The system is integrated into the curricula of courses in English, Biology, Anthropology, Political Science, and Medicine [74]. 'In Memoriam' is an application of Intermedia.

Tennyson's *In Memoriam* is a particularly complex, mid-Victorian poem that was an attempt to create new versions of traditional major poetic forms from separate sections. Each section is a poem that can stand on its own. It is particularly appropriate for hypertext representation as it makes extensive use of echoing, allusion, and repetition. Tennyson's entire poem was placed in Intermedia and linked to:

*   variant readings from manuscripts;
*   published critical commentary; and

- passages from works by other authors.

In the subsequent months, members of a graduate seminar added more than 100 documents, each commenting specifically on one or more sections of the poem and on one another's work. The first assignment for the project required them to create five documents to append to individual sections of the poem. Each week members of the seminar read the contributions of others, added more documents, and then made links. The final assignment of the project involved students putting online the texts of poems by another poet that had obvious relevance to individual sections of Tennyson's work. Throughout the class students felt they benefited from the opportunity to interact through Intermedia with one another.

Videoconferencing and hypermedia, despite huge amounts of publicity, are not yet common in classrooms. This may be due to harsh financial pressures on educational institutions. However, there have been some notable experiments with relatively *inexpensive technologies*. The Department of Geography at Boston University has experimented with several phone-based, undergraduate courses [3]. The novel, phone-based elements for the classes are telephone conferencing, asynchronous and real-time computer conferencing, electronic mail within and beyond campus, and the use of data bases and external networks for research.

Teleconferences are simpler and initially more engaging than computer conferences. For most students, the most successful and popular element of these classes is the part that is technologically simplest: the use of a speakerphone to enliven class sessions with outside guests. This is done by plugging a speakerphone into a regular phone jack and making a prearranged, long-distance call.

Guests are selected on the basis of complementary expertise or 'real world' experience. Despite some initial awkwardness, most guests express pleasure at the opportunity to interact with bright college students who are interested in what they are doing. Discussion with the guest usually lasts about an hour. Most of these talks were planned and arranged beforehand in accordance with the structure of the course syllabus. However, some themes develop a life of their own. For example, after a lecture and readings on rainforest issues, the class interviewed a distinguished tropical ecologist who is helping to develop an international Biosphere between Costa Rica and Panama. This *discussion* in turn raised a new set of issues about the politics of conservation. The class then spoke with a leader in Costa Rica, who articulately explained why he bitterly opposes the formation of an international Biosphere.

The management of the course, assignment giving, and considerable interaction between instructor and students was conducted through a semester-long *computer conference*. Class members exchanged information in an organized fashion through the campus computer system and personal computers that were connected to the campus through modems and outside phone lines.

The course was structured so that major syllabus topics were introduced by lectures, class discussions, and the long-distance speakerphone presentations. Topics such as deforestation, coastal resource management, and sustainable agriculture were then set up as subconferences. Students kept individual *subconferences* running by adding comments to the particular subconferences, raising questions and carrying on student-to-student debate, and writing short critiques of assigned readings and of each other's work. As students became more skillful network users, they would reinforce some subconferences by importing relevant material from the hundreds of other conferences on the electronic highways. Often, vast amounts of highly up-to-date, technical material could be found that would carry the discussion far beyond the initial class presentation.

At the outset of the semester, students tend to participate in these conferences somewhat passively. They relate to them as if they were books — reading messages, taking notes, and sometimes importing ('downloading') information for general use within the class-only conference. Gradually, however, they learn that they can 'talk back' from their keyboards; and they begin to engage more aggressively in two-way communication. For more mature students — in particular, the graduate students in environmental studies — the course structure fades into the backdrop as they begin to relate more directly to their *self-discovered communities* of common interest. Typically, their energies are captured by conference participation and the requirement to produce an original paper.

A *virtual reality* was created by a graduate student who applied her background in tropical ecology and computer programming to construct the shell and initial biological population for a 'virtual rainforest'. This is a text-based simulation of a rainforest environment, something like the popular adventure games on personal computers. In this case, a 'player' receives messages something like, "You hear a fluttering screech and look up through the green canopy where you see a troupe of howler monkeys . . ." Although kinetically less dramatic to students than the competition in video arcades, such 'games' are intriguing for several reasons. They can be freely accessed through the Internet from virtually any networked campus computer, they can accommodate hundreds of players in real time who are working interactively within the created environment. Their educational content could be developed in highly sophisticated ways by succeeding generations of players and rainforest makers. For example, the plant and animal population of the 'virtual rainforest' could be biologically expanded; the forest could be populated by slash-and-burn farmers, cattle ranchers, and ecotourism operators; and so on.

Although low cost virtual reality can be achieved with textual bulletin boards, visually enticing, collaborative, educational games have also been created. *Virtual museums* and even cities have been built (see Figure 2.6). Through these virtual realities, students can interact with one another and learn about the environment and one another.

Outside of the networked Virtual Art Museum, which is designed to resemble the College of Fine Arts, Carnegie Mellon University. Object in front is a UFO, or flying saucer, which can be piloted by end users. Produced for Expedition 92, Germany. Designed by Carl Eugene Loeffler

Figure 2.6: *Virtual Museum.* The networked Virtual Art Museum, is designed to resemble the College of Fine Arts at Carnegie Mellon University. The object in front is a UFO, or flying saucer, which can be piloted by end users. This virtual reality was designed by Carl Eugene Loeffler and the image comes from the World Wide Web site: www.nta.no/telektronikk/4.93.dir.

2.8   Conclusion

Evidence shows that teams of people are needed to effectively develop courseware [120]. The expertise represented in the team should include a content matter specialist, an instructional designer, and a programmer. The use of a *team* not only makes it more likely that all areas of expertise will be adequately represented, but also provides insurance against the errors and bias of one individual appearing in the final product [116].

The development of courseware needs to be somehow coordinated. Coordination can be defined as the act of working together harmoniously. *Coordination Theory* is a body of principles describing how this can be achieved with respect to how activities can be coordinated or how people can work together harmoniously.

In large-scale production of courseware, authors work as members of teams. People come together with complementary skills, and these skills must be mapped onto appropriate roles. The physical environment of a group, its size, and the proximity of members are factors that can influence the quality of communication and, therefore,coordination.

If one can successfully model a group process, then one can better predict the behavior of the group, and, more importantly, from the computer scientist perspective, one can imagine computer tools which can play an active role in the group process. A modeling language for group communication and coordination, the *AME modeling language,* uses roles, messages, functions, and activities. The courseware production manager will need to have an overall view of the progress of each of the constitutive elements within the courseware cycle, to make judgments about resource availability and completion dates. The courseware development cycle must therefore contain the tools or at least the interface to the tools needed by the manager to facilitate the communication between himself and the other team members. A model for the coordination of a team of courseware developers is presented in Chapter 7 via the AME modeling language.

Having understood the factors which contribute to group success, one can ask 'what kind of technology might best support group processes'? Computer-mediated communication relies on networks of computers to support people in synchronous and asynchronous interactions. The information technology that is particularly designed for supporting group work is called *groupware,* and the use of groupware leads to computer-supported collaborative work. A wide range of groupware systems has been implemented that extends from those which basically facilitate the sharing of text in databases to those which give distant users direct audio and visual contact with one another.

Collaborative learning has been introduced in this chapter by way of illustrating both how the principles of coordination can apply to student learning and how students can participate in courseware development. The focus of the book is on the development of courseware, and in the modern, interactive, technology-supported classroom and world, students can easily, directly, contribute to the development of courseware. Managing this contribution requires a clear understanding of the principles of coordination and of education.

Organizations are striving to become more responsive both to their customers and their staff. This leads to the virtual organization — an organization which is not tied to a particular physical location and is open all the time. Coordination is the highest level and most important activity in any organization, and is particularly critical to the success of a virtual organization. The amazing growth in the use of information technology and telecommunications has increased the possibilities for technologically-supported coordination across space and time boundaries. An understanding of coordination theory and tools helps an organization assume the desirable properties of a virtual organization.

3
Reuse

For many years courseware authors have tried to determine the factors that influence the efficiency of courseware development. Reusable, instructional templates were identified as contributing to efficient courseware authoring over 15 years ago [4]. As the availability of courseware templates or components has increased, the attractiveness of building and exploiting libraries of these components has grown.

The *vision for reuse* is to move from the current 'reinvent the courseware' cycle to a library-based way of constructing courseware [34]. A conceptual framework for reuse should provide the technological and management basis to influence and enable this paradigm shift. In this new paradigm the standard approach to courseware development is to derive systems principally from existing assets rather than to create the systems anew. Reusable assets are thus a central concept of the reuse vision, and they imply a need for processes to create such assets, manage them, and utilize them to produce new systems.

3.1   The Need

Reusable information can take many forms, such as a library of software routines included in a computer program, or a standard letter used by a company to offer the same services to a number of customers. Approaches to *courseware reuse* center on multiple access points into libraries of teaching material and the ability to reassemble components [108]. The goal is to create new courses which are combinations of pre-existing ones.

Often in industrial situations courseware must be developed to cover a number of different applications. This may be because the courseware must describe:

*   a number of slightly different products, each of which shares a number of common components, or
*   the material in different ways to suit different types of student, with differing needs and abilities.

For example when developing instructional material for a new series of aircraft, it will be necessary to describe various systems and subsystems at various levels of detail. The theory, construction, operation and maintenance of an *aeroengine* would need to be included to various levels of detail creating a whole range of different courses. The description of an aeroengine may for instance require a description of what the pilot, the air engineer, or the ground technician specifically need to know (see Figure 3.1). This is not the only possible breakdown, another might be based on the operation being described, rather than the student (see Figure 3.2).

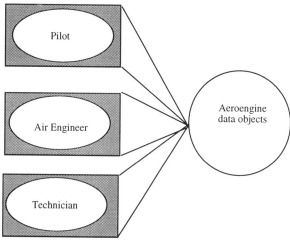

Figure 3.1: *Aeroengine Objects One.* The description of an aeroengine may require a number of different objects, each of which describe the concepts in a way appropriate for specific roles.

The use of a single *repository* of course material on the aeroengine means that when changes are made (even the complete replacement of the engine by another design) the material that must be amended is available in a single, locatable place. The individual courseware items can be designed and written by subject and media specialists who fully understand the issues that need to be taught, and then integrated into the final course by the course designer, who takes the available materials, commissioning amendments or additional modules as necessary to produce the required course. In cases where there are alternatives as to which material should be included, such as, for instance, when the airline purchasing the aircraft specifies one of a number of alternative engines, it is possible to ensure that the correct material is included from the courseware components available.

The development effort required to produce courseware is substantial. In the aerospace training sector, one company spends about *400 hours* in developing each hour of training material [103]. The inclusion of high quality sound, animation, or video can mean that developing a course from which students gain 1 hour of training

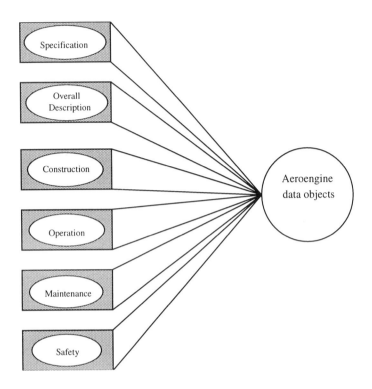

Figure 3.2: *Aeroengine Objects Two.* The description of the engine is categorized in terms of the different functions required from the engine.

time will require *800 hours* from the authors of the courseware [16].

In a film, the production of a single frame often costs over $300. Amazingly this ultraexpensive footage is only used once. The million dollar scene has its place in the movie, and that is the only place it will be seen.

Several efforts have been made to build *video libraries* which could be reused. The MIT Media Laboratory experimented with repurposing footage from the soap opera *Dallas* for interactive replay. The experiment failed because this apparently multithreaded soap opera was too tightly structured to be repurposed [98].

The MIT Media Laboratory has a toolset for building multiuse video databases. The toolset includes a database browsing tool, a story generation tool, and a visual editing tool. The *visual editing tool* allows descriptions to be attached to any group of contiguous frames of video and also allows for layered descriptions. Thus any group of frames may have a number of descriptions associated with it. This allows the video to be described at different granularities and in different contexts [42].

Libraries of media are being made available for reuse in various projects. For instance, the University of Bristol has produced a videodisc with 36,000 biomedical images. Copyright of the images remains with the donors of the images. The images can, however, be freely reused for nonprofit making purposes. A text catalogue of the material is available and can be searched with a free text retrieval system [148].

The increasing interest in reusable courseware is being matched by an increase in research on the topic. Many unanswered questions remain, such as how to structure hypermedia courseware for effective reuse and how to coordinate people for the creation of libraries. The software reuse community is years ahead of the hypermedia courseware community and might have partial answers.

3.2   Software Reuse

Software reuse is a field that has been studied by researchers since the 1960s. A conference held in 1968 by NATO focused on the software crisis — the problem of building large, reliable software systems in a controlled, cost-effective way. As the demand for cost-effective software rises, reuse becomes increasingly important as a potential solution to low programmer productivity.

One fundamental weakness in software creation is that new software systems are usually entirely constructed *from scratch* [82]. Over and over again, programmers weave a number of basic patterns: sorting, searching, reading, writing, comparing, traversing, allocating and synchronizing. Attempts have been made to measure this phenomenon. One estimate is that less than 15% of new code serves an original purpose. Another study done at the Missile Systems Division of the Raytheon Company observed that 40-60% of actual program code was repeated in more than one application. Further studies have shown that more than 60% of the software development effort goes into developing newer versions of existing programs [117].

A number of tools and methods to support the creation of component libraries have been investigated. One such example is the Reusable Software Library (RSL) [19], developed by Intermetrics. The RSL's software classification scheme and its database of software attributes have been designed to ease the selection of reusable components. More importantly, the RSL's tools help software developers to find and evaluate components that meet their requirements. These library tools have been integrated with software design tools, making reuse a natural extension of the design process. Still more tools automate the work of the librarian, who must enter the components' attributes into the database and maintain the RSL. Another example of a software library is IMSL [64], which is a mathematics library with components hierarchically classified by abstract computational or analytical capabilities.

3.3   One Reuse Framework

One framework for reuse consists of dual, interconnected 'process idioms' called Reuse Management and Reuse Engineering (see Figure 3.3). The Framework is *generic* with respect to domains, organizations, and technologies. Framework concepts should generally be applicable to reuse in any information-intensive context. The scope is limited to identifying the processes involved in reuse and describing at a high level how those processes operate and interact.

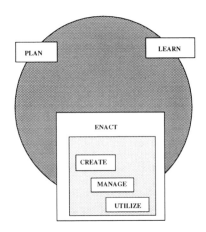

Figure 3.3: *Reuse Management and Reuse Engineering.* Plan, Enact, and Learn are in the Management idiom. Create, Manage and Utilize are in the Engineering idiom.

The Framework described here is largely based on a document entitled "STARS Conceptual Framework for Reuse Processes" [13]. That document reflects an effort to modernize software productivity by the *Software Technology for Adaptable, Reliable Systems* (STARS) program of the U.S. Department of Defense (see Figure 3.4). The Framework reflects the experiences of information reuse efforts both within and outside of STARS. For an organization undertaking a reuse program, the Framework must be augmented and numerous documents provide information for such an augmentation [37][135][136][144].

Naturally, other organizations also have reuse frameworks. For instance, the *North Atlantic Treaty Organization* has published a three-volume standard for software reuse [50][51][52]. The volumes are entitled:

- *Development of Reusable Software Components,*
- *Management of a Reusable Software Component Library,* and
- *Software Reuse Procedures.*

The content of these 3 volumes is in principle harmonious with the content of the 'Conceptual Framework for Reuse' of STARS.

3.3.1   Reuse Management

Reuse involves both *people* and *information*. The Reuse Management process idiom focuses on people and describes a cyclical pattern of planning, enacting, and learning (see Figure 3.5). Reuse Management incorporates emerging general theories of organizational learning [126] that have been adapted to the reuse-based context. The immediately following subsections deal with managing people, but later this chapter will emphasize the information side of reuse under the headings of Asset Creation, Asset Management, and Asset Utilization.

The *Reuse Planning* process encompasses both strategic planning and tactical, project-oriented planning within a reuse program. One key strategic reuse planning function, which augments traditional product line planning within an organization, is to select the key domains of focus for the reuse program and determine how the domain assets will support the organization's product engineering efforts. One key focus of Reuse Planning is the reuse infrastructure that is required to sustain a reuse-based approach. The outputs from the Reuse Planning include:

- Plans for the reuse program, and
- Committed resources to support the projects, in terms of staff and equipment.

The five processes in planning are Assessment, Direction Setting, Scoping, Infrastructure Planning, and Project Planning.

Assessment processes characterize the current state of reuse practice within an organization, the readiness of the organization as a whole for practicing reuse, and the reuse technology and expertise available. *Direction Setting* processes define specific objectives for the reuse program, strategies for achieving those objectives, and criteria for evaluating how successfully the objectives have been met. Scoping processes define the overall scope of the reuse program by delineating the program's technical and organizational boundaries.

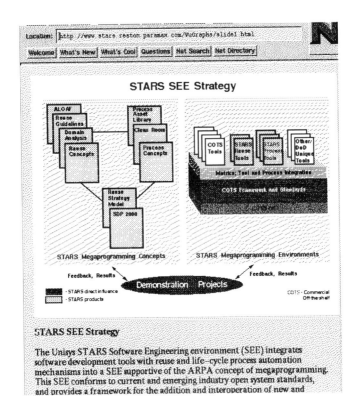

Figure 3.4: *STARS Strategy*: This window on the World Wide Web site www.stars.reston.paramax.com/VuGraphs/slide1.html shows the extensive program of reuse pursued by the Department of Defense in its STARS initiative. Megaprogramming concepts are merged with megaprogramming environments through demonstration projects.

A first step in domain selection is to identify and characterize promising candidate domains, based on the organization's business interests and key areas of expertise. Criteria for identifying promising domains include [63]:

• The domain is well-understood, and
• The domain reusable assets will not become obsolete before the investment in their development can be recovered.

Infrastructure Planning processes identify needs for various types of support that are common among planned reuse projects, and develop plans for establishing a shared reuse infrastructure to satisfy those needs. *Project Planning* is responsible for establishing specific objectives for each identified project, and for defining the metrics to be used to evaluate the effectiveness of the projects relative to those objectives. A variety of metrics can be defined relating specifically to assets and reuse, such as:

- The percentage of each application product that was directly derived from domain assets,
- The number of times each asset has been reused, and
- The number of regular users of an asset library.

The final stage of Project Planning is to plan the reuse project's resource needs, budgets, and schedules in detail and then obtain the necessary commitment to implement the plans. Commitment should be obtained from both higher level management and the technical staff members whose buy-in will ultimately determine whether or not reuse practice is really improved by the program.

Reuse Enactment addresses initiation, performance, and retirement of the various reuse-related plans. *Reuse Enactment* includes Project Management processes and Infrastructure Implementation processes. *Project Management processes* establish a temporal context for reuse project activities and include the following specific functional areas:

- Project initiation activities include allocation and tailoring of technical reuse infrastructure capabilities to specific projects.
- Project performance is where the processes being enacted are actually performed by individual staff members.
- Project control activities intervene with project performance to optimize overall project performance relative to project objectives.
- Project monitoring activities capture information from the projects as they are performed.
- Project retirement activities include terminating the project and archiving the key results.

Infrastructure Implementation processes ensure that reuse infrastructure capabilities are established and evolved in accordance with project needs. The goal of *Reuse Learning* processes is to enhance the performance of a reuse program. The results of Reuse Learning are fed back to Reuse Planning processes in the form of recommendations for the next reuse program cycle.

REUSE MANAGEMENT
- Planning
    - Assessment
    - Direction Setting
    - Scoping
    - Infrastructure Planning
    - Project Planning
- Enacting
    - Project Management
    - Infrastructure Implementation
- Learning
    - Project Observation
    - Project Evaluation
    - Innovation Exploration
    - Enhancement Recommendation

Figure 3.5: *Reuse Management.* Planning, Enacting, and Learning include the processes listed above.

3.3.2   Asset Creation

Reuse Engineering addresses the creation, management, and utilization of reusable assets. Asset Management serves a brokerage role between Asset Creation and Asset Utilization and reflects common marketplace interactions (see Figure 3.6). In an organization that has a mature reuse program underway, there will likely be multiple Asset Creation, Asset Management, and Asset Utilization projects in operation simultaneously.

The goals of *Asset Creation* are to capture, organize, and represent knowledge about a domain, and use that knowledge to develop reusable assets. Asset Creation can be viewed as consisting of:

1.   Domain Modeling processes that characterize application products in terms of what the products have in common and how they vary, and
2.   Asset Implementation processes that produce reusable assets.

Domain models and asset bases are logically at different levels of abstraction and serve different purposes. The primary role of domain models within Asset Creation is to assist in determining which asset should be produced and the range of characteristics they should support. For that reason, domain models focus on describing the commonality and variability among systems, rather than on describing the systems themselves. The assets that are developed using the domain models are at a lower level of abstraction, they implement products.

- Asset Creation
  - Domain Analysis and Modeling
  - Domain Architecture Development
  - Asset Implementation
- Asset Management
  - Library Operation
  - Library Data Modeling
  - Library Usage Support
  - Asset Brokering
  - Asset Acquisition
  - Asset Acceptance
  - Asset Cataloging
  - Asset Certification
- Asset Utilization
  - Asset Criteria Determination
  - Asset Identification
  - Asset Selection
  - Asset Tailoring
  - Asset Integration

Figure 3.6: *Decomposition of Reuse Engineering.* The three main processes of engineering reusable assets; namely, creation, management, and utilization, are shown here with their many subprocesses.

Domain analysis processes have in common the following general activities [136][33]:

- Reverse engineering,
- Knowledge acquisition,
- Technology forecasting,
- Domain modeling, and
- Asset specification.

To extract expertise already encoded in existing information products they may be analyzed using reverse engineering techniques. Processes to support knowledge acquisition in domain analysis can be adapted from knowledge acquisition techniques used for in-depth interviewing in any discipline.

In order for reuse to remain viable over a period of years so that a return on the investment in asset creation will be fully realized, forecasting of future trends is essential. Then an organization can accommodate changes in a manner that will allow smooth evolution and modernization of assets over time. If knowledge acquisition is a craft, *technology forecasting* is an art. Short-term forecasts of a few months can often be developed with reasonable confidence. Long-term forecasts of several years are difficult to develop with confidence.

After the gathering of domain information by reverse engineering, knowledge acquisition, and forecasting, the information is integrated into domain models that can be used to support asset specification and development. This is usually done in an ad hoc manner because general methods do not adequately support comprehensive model synthesis of this nature. Domain models need to be validated in some way to establish confidence in their correctness and utility. Processes supporting *model validation* include walkthroughs, expert reviews, and trial application of assets derived from the models.

The goal of *Asset Implementation* is to produce the assets in the asset base. This could be done by creating the assets from scratch with guidance from the domain models as to what kinds of components should be developed. Alternately, a company may require that its information developers provide whatever information they develop to the reuse librarians so that it can be considered for incorporation into the library. This latter case in which libraries acquire existing components is discussed in the next sections.

3.3.3   Asset Management

Asset Management processes fall into two general classes: processes that focus on acquiring, installing, and evaluating individual assets in a library, and processes that focus on developing and operating libraries that house collections of assets, provide access to those assets, and support their utilization (see Figure 3.7). Asset Management overlaps in some ways with Reuse Management. Organizational assets, such as plans, are generally treated as part of the reuse infrastructure, whereas library support technology is generally considered the province of Asset Management. Asset Management addresses the selection and support of technology that is inherently asset-, library-, or domain-specific, or tailored to be so.

A library houses managed asset collections. A library need not be automated to effectively manage a collection of assets and serve a useful mediator role between Asset Creation and Asset Utilization processes. The goal of *Library Operation processes* is to ensure the availability and accessibility of the library and its associated assets for Asset Utilization. This can involve a variety of activities, such as:

- Administration and operation of the physical library facility,
- Library access control and security,
- Periodic archiving and backup of library contents, and

• Support for interoperation with other libraries.

These activities are strictly operational in nature, and organizations may consider them to be aspects of general infrastructure. However, there are aspects of these activities that relate specifically to asset libraries and merit attention from an Asset Management perspective. Some typical library user roles, corresponding to some of the Asset Management and Asset Utilization processes, include library data modeler, asset cataloger, asset certifier, library operator, asset utilizer, and asset broker.

The goal of *Library Data Modeling processes* is to develop a data model for describing assets within a library. This library data model synthesizes the domain models, asset models, and assets. The specific approach is thus dependent on the characteristics of the Asset Creation products and on the objectives of the library in supporting Asset Utilization. If the library's objectives are to provide a basic search and retrieval capability for individual assets, it should suffice for the library data model to include mainly taxonomic information derived from one or more domain models. If the objectives are more ambitious, then the library data model must integrate additional elements of the domain models. In addition to incorporating information produced by Asset Creation processes, the library data model also codifies information that specifically addresses Asset Management needs. For example, a model could include data elements to record asset certification information and user feedback data.

In addition to simply operating a library and making assets available within it, Asset Management should provide a set of library services that anticipate and address specific asset utilizer needs. Examples of these kinds of services include:

• the collection and generation of asset data in a number of different formats, including a variety of media (e.g., paper and online files), and
• the operation of electronic hot lines to accept and resolve user complaints.

Specific tools can support activities such as viewing assets, extracting sets of closely related assets, and so on. An often critical form of *Library Usage Support* is direct, personal assistance to users. These consultation services can be likened to the role of the traditional librarian in conventional book libraries. Such services can be automated to some degree, but may be most effective when rendered in person. This person-to-person approach can effectively lower the technological barriers to reuse that typical library software presents to many users.

Related to activities considered library processes are *asset processes*. These include asset brokering, asset acquisition, asset acceptance, asset cataloging, and asset certification [13]. Localized efforts may monitor asset flows, interactions, and feedback among Asset Creation, Management, and Utilization processes, and apply that knowledge to work proactively with all concerned parties to improve effectiveness in particular areas. Such activities can be viewed as *Asset Brokering processes.*

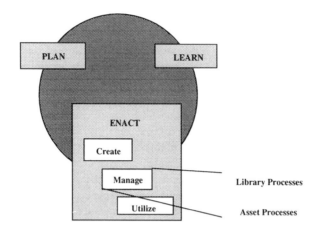

Figure 3.7: *Managing Engineering.* The reuse cycle is shown with detail provided for the Management phase in which Library and Asset processes occur.

The principal goal of *Asset Acquisition* is to obtain assets from external sources to support Asset Utilization activities. Asset Acquisition obtains assets that appear to be good candidates for inclusion in an asset library. The goal of *Asset Acceptance* is to ensure that an asset that is a candidate for inclusion in a library satisfies relevant policy, legal, and domain-specific constraints. The purpose of library policy constraints is typically to ensure that assets in a library satisfy at least minimal criteria for quality and suitability for use in Asset Utilization activities. *Asset Cataloging* incorporates accepted assets into a library by classifying, describing, and installing them. Asset certification goes beyond asset acceptance and puts the 'official seal of approval' on an asset after rigorous testing.

3.3.4   Asset Utilization

he goal of Asset Utilization is to construct new application products using previously developed assets. The outputs from Asset Utilization include:

- Information products that are constructed from assets,
- New assets for incorporation into the asset base, and

• Feedback concerning the library and its assets.

Asset Utilization generally involves determining a set of criteria to use in selecting assets for reuse, identifying suitable candidate assets in the context of those criteria, selecting and tailoring assets to meet the criteria, and integrating the tailored assets with the target application.

The reuser must tailor assets that have been selected for reuse so that they satisfy target system requirements. This tailoring generally comes in two forms, either or both of which may be applied to any given asset:

• *Anticipated Target* system needs lie within the range of variability anticipated for an asset during Asset Creation; the asset encapsulates the variability through some set of 'parameters'.
• *Unanticipated Target* system needs lie outside the range of variability anticipated for an asset during Asset Creation. There is a need for new features where no variability was anticipated.

To perform *anticipated tailoring,* an engineer must understand the range of variability an asset may accommodate and how the asset's parameters are used to select among the variations. This information should be included in the library in the form of 'reuse instructions' for the asset, which may be augmented by examples. In addition to parameterization, another technique that can be used for anticipated tailoring is hand modification of the asset in accordance with precise instructions. An asset that can be tailored in this manner is typically called a *template.*

Unanticipated tailoring is more of an ad hoc process in which the reuser assesses the asset's shortcomings relative to system needs and then employs whichever strategies are appropriate to tailor the asset to those needs. This often involves hand modification of the asset to add desired features or remove undesired features.

3.4   Another Reuse Framework

Another view of a reuse lifecycle shows three phases:

1   Organizing,
2   Retrieving, and
3   Reorganizing.

Courseware materials must be somehow *organized* before they can be successfully reused. Given a partial description of a desired course, the organization of existing courseware material may serve as a guide in *retrieving* the relevant components. Finally, the candidate objects must be *reorganized* so as to produce the new course.

3.4.1   Organizing

Learning materials for a particular subject communicate some model of the world, and for reuse purposes, one will need access to this model. Word patterns and outlines are inherent in courseware and provide models of the subject domain. The *outline* manifests itself in the layout of the course as highlighted and numbered headings in the body of the course, as well as in a separate listing at the beginning of the course. This physical layout helps people understand the logical structure of the course and find thematically organized sections in the course [83].

The analogue of a 'table of contents' for a single course in a large, course collection is a *thesaurus* or indexing language. Although a thesaurus, in the lay use of the word, usually suggests an alphabetically sorted list of terms and their attached synonyms, in the library science field this is often a greatly expanded idea. A thesaurus is a set of concepts in which each individual concept is represented with synonymous terms and broader, narrower, and related concepts [86]. The thesaurus covers a large, multifaceted library of courses in a kind of object-oriented way. A thesaurus may be presented in a hierarchical, 'table of contents' form.

3.4.2   Retrieving

Once courses have been organized, sophisticated strategies can be applied for retrieving course components. Given the goal of creating a course based on a partial description, one general strategy is to:

*   find the closest match between the partial description and the contents of the library, and
*   determine how much of the partial description can be completed by copying from the library.

Course components can be *retrieved* based on the words contained within them or their outline headings. A search engine can operate on a more complex level than simply retrieving files containing a particular word. The words of the index can be combined with logical operations such as union, intersection or complement. The outline provides the user with a simple way to find specific sections of interest, as the hierarchical structure facilitates moving in a top-down fashion from the general to the more specific. Mappings from one course's outline to another can be exploited to find more information.

A thesaurus supports searching via concepts or their relations, such as 'broader-than'. For example, if the user asks for course components about *'graph traversal'* but the system has no course components indexed with that term, then the system might find the term closest to 'graph traversal' in the thesaurus and perform retrieval on that term. In this case, in the thesaurus, 'graph algorithms' is a broader concept than 'graph traversal', and if the retrieval system has course components indexed under 'graph algorithms', then the system should return those course components (see Figure 3.8). The thesaurus may also help connect outlines or objects by indexing different course components with the same thesaurus term. *Metathesauri* may connect concepts from one thesaurus with those in another and thus support retrieval across different course databases, each with its own individual thesaurus [106]. A partial description in terms of attribute values of an object could guide the search for another object with similar attributes.

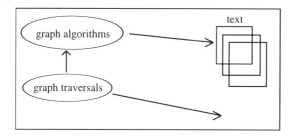

USER: text on 'graph traversals
SYSTEM: none on 'graph traversals
3 on broader concept 'graph algorithms'

Figure 3.8: *Guaranteed Return.* The user has requested text on 'graph traversals', and the thesaurus has been followed to find related text.

3.4.3   Reorganizing

The goal of reuse is not to find information but rather to actually create a new product. The retrieved information does not, by itself, constitute a new product, as the information must be reorganized or tailored [87]. Preexistent connections among components may be exploited in this reorganization phase. *Reorganization* is typically performed by a course expert who will need to ensure that there is a proper progression in the material, and no material is missing.

If a course is organized in a consistent manner, this then lends itself to reuse [108]. As an example, if a course were organized along the lines of a list of the attributes of different types of mammals, with components of analogous material in each section, then simply *traversing* the database in a different manner would enable the material to be reorganized with a different emphasis (see Figure 3.9).

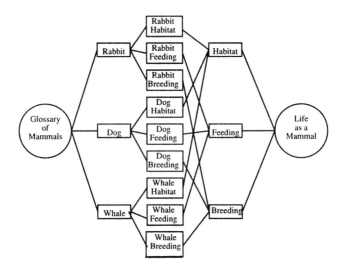

Figure 3.9: *New Edges.* This diagram represents how knowledge components can provide a different message when a simple reorganization mechanism traverses them from right to left rather than from left to right.

A different example concerns a set of courses which must follow the same outline at levels 1 and 2; for example, the level-1 Section 'Project Plan' must contain the level-2 Sections:

2.1   Technical Approach and
2.2   Work Breakdown Structure.

Given a collection of such courses, then *recombining* parts into a new course can be done by first collecting level-3 sections that have particular words in them. These level-3 sections may then be combined into a new course such that the level-3 sections remain attached to their appropriate level-2 sections (see Figure 3.10).

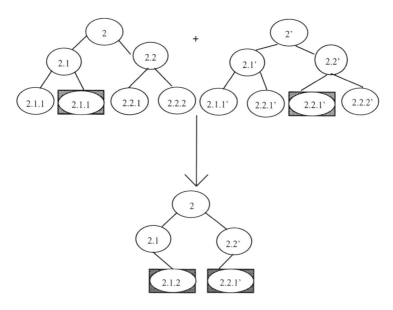

Figure 3.10: *Reorganization of Course.* From the two course outlines in the top half of the figure several sections have been identified as relevant to the user's interest and are enclosed in squares. They are recombined into one course at the bottom by maintaining the overall network architecture but pruning the unwanted sections.

3.5   Costs

Software reuse is difficult for companies to initiate because it has the least desirable cost structure, initially very high, recouping over time. *Startup costs* include training staff to set up the library, populating the library, and training the development teams to use the library. Gradual returns over the life of the library should pay for initial costs over a period of time, and return profits, but may not. There are other possible benefits in the quality of the new products and minimization of developer time and resources, but these benefits may be difficult to measure (see Figure 3.11).

The method used to estimate *reuse costs and benefits* should be compatible with the methods used by the rest of the institution. The two quantities of primary importance are:

- the net saving to the individual user for each instance of reuse of a component and
- the net saving to the company from all reuses of the component.

The quantities in the analysis can be expressed either in some monetary unit or in labor hours. The savings due to reuse, SR, is the sum of costs avoided each time the component is reused [51].

Related to savings are service life and demand:

- The service life, L, is the useful lifetime of the component in years.
- Demand, is the number N, of times the component is likely to be used during its service life. If the costs and benefits may vary from year to year, then the demand should be apportioned per year as Ny where y = 1, 2, ..., L.

The costs associated with a component may be formalized as:

- The cost to reuse, C_R, is the cost incurred each time the component is reused, including retrieval and tailoring costs.
- The accession time, T_A, is the amount of time between the decision to acquire the component and its availability in the library.
- The accession cost, C_A, is the cost to add the component to the library.
- The maintenance cost, C_M, is the cost to maintain the component in the library. If yearly costs vary, the maintenance cost distribution C_{My} where y=1, 2, ..., L is the cost to maintain the component for each year of its service life.

The *net saving* NSR to the individual for each instance of reuse is the difference between the saving due to avoided cost and the cost to reuse, or in symbols, NSR = S_R - C_R. The total savings from all instances of reuse is NSR multiplied by the number of reuses. Thus the net savings from all reuses NSP is the total saving minus the accession and maintenance costs, or in symbols, NSP = (NSR x N) - (C_A + C_M).

NSP may be calculated on an annual basis. For each year, NSP_y = (NSR x N_y) - C_{My}. This calculation assumes that the accession cost is incurred prior to the beginning of the first year of service and is recorded separately. The cost estimation method may include an adjustment for the fact that future cash flows decrease in value with time at a rate that can be given the discount rate i. Thus the annual discounted NSP can be given as

$$DNSP_y = ((NSR \times N_y) - C_{My}) / (1 + i)^y.$$

To compare two potential reusable components to determine which to acquire for the library and which not, the *cumulative discounted cash flow* CDCF for each would be determined and the component would be preferred with the higher CDCF. CDCF = $DNSP_1 + DNSP_2 + ... + DNSP_L - C_A$. With the appropriate data and these formulas, a company can better plan its reuse investments.

Depending on the management strategy adopted by the developer company, the costs of reuse may be absorbed by the developer in the hope of creating similar projects later, and thus recouping the investment that way. Or alternatively the developer may form a *partnership with the client,* where initial startup costs and any later benefits are both shared.

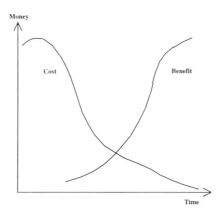

Figure 3.11: *Reuse Costs.* Initially the cost of the reuse program is very high, as the library of reusable items is built. Returns cannot start until the library is usable, and then will tend to be low, as the library needs to become suited to the developers who use it and gaps in the libraries content are filled. The final level of return is uncertain, it should become high and remain high, but this will depend on the quality of the reuse library, its retrieval system and the willingness of developers to reuse.

3.6   Copyright

Through *courseware reuse,* assets which have been developed for one purpose are used to produce new courseware. The courseware components have developers and authors, who own the material, and from whom permission must be sought, if components are to be reused. Some organizations own their own material and the subject of copyright is not an issue in these circumstances. However, when one organization wishes to reuse the material from another organization to develop courseware, permission must be sought.

3.6.1   The Law Concerning Copyright

The Copyright Act of 1956 says that

> *Ideas are free but a man's expression of his ideas is his own property.*

The purpose of copyright is to reward the author, to encourage the development of cultural, scientific and educational works, and to encourage dissemination and exploitation of this material by protecting the investments of those, such as publishers, who enable this dissemination and exploitation to take place [10]. Authors have rights in the work they produce. Those who make a sound recording or film have rights in the recording or the film. Owners of rights who are protected under the *Copyright Act* include:

*   authors, composers, artists, photographers, publishers, and
*   makers of sound recordings and video tapes.

The maker of a *sound recording* or a *video tape* has a copyright in the sound recording or video tape that is separate and distinct from, and in addition to, the copyright in the material contained in the sound recording or video tape. The owner of rights in a sound recording is the person who owns the sound recording at the time when it is made. The owner of the rights in a video tape will, in practice, be the person or institution making the arrangements for the sound and vision to be recorded. There is no specific reference to video recording in the Copyright Act of 1956 or in international conventions, but the majority opinion is that a video tape owner of rights in a recording may or may not also hold the copyright on the material in the recording, for this is something quite distinct; and he may or may not be concerned with the rights of the performers who take part in the recording.

Authors can control the following in relation to their copyright works:

*   reproduction, including recording and filming;
*   publishing;
*   performance in public;
*   broadcasting;

- causing the work to be transmitted to the subscribers to a diffusion service;
- adapting, translating, or arranging; and
- doing, in relation to an adoption of the work, any of the other acts mentioned above.

Authors usually transfer all or part of their rights in a work to a *publisher* or agent who is responsible for making the work available to the public and for safeguarding the rights involved. The intention of the Copyright Act is clear. Copyright material in any media cannot be reproduced or copied, in whole or in part, without the permission of all those who hold rights in it.

3.6.2   Exceptions to Cover Every Day Use

Some copying is necessary in ordinary business. To provide for this, exceptions are made to the Copyright Act and in some instances a limited amount of copying is not an infringement of copyright but is fair dealing. A student or research worker may often need a copy of a text for working purposes. A critic reviewing a book, a film, or a television program, may need to cite passages to illustrate his points. A newspaper may need to quote passages from a text in order to report current events. The Copyright Act recognizes that such copying is necessary, but leaves the courts to decide what constitutes 'fair dealing'.

The Society of Authors and the Publishers Association have issued a joint statement to indicate what they consider to be reasonable limits of fair dealing. They state that:

> No fair dealing with literary material shall constitute an infringement of the copyright in the work if it is for the purposes of criticism or review, whether of that work or of another work, and is accompanied by a sufficient acknowledgment.

Sufficient acknowledgment is defined as an acknowledgment identifying the work in question by its title and author. The Society of Authors and the Publishers Association are agreed in expressing the view that objection could not normally be taken to the quotation in a book or article for purposes of criticism or review of:

> a single extract up to 400 words, or a series of extracts (with comments interposed) up to a total of 800 words but of which no one extract exceeds 300 words.

3.7   Interchange

Interchange of information between various systems is vital in order to reuse that information. Some authors and readers are currently reluctant to use hypermedia because of the incompatibilities among the many different hypermedia systems. For instance, when an author prepares a hypermedia document in one system, a reader who only uses a different system will not be able to read that author's work. This *incompatibility* severely restricts the dissemination of hypermedia.

3.7.1   Standards

As long as platforms continue to be distinguished by differing abilities to process various media, there will continue to be good technical reasons for having native media formats that are closely matched to platform-dependent interfaces. If one is a user of a certain tool, then, in theory, one can create and access information in any format that the tool supports. In practice, there are often problems in interchanging information with others, even if one only uses a different version of the tool or has different platforms or environments where one runs it (e.g., different installed fonts). If one wants to give information to someone who does not use the tool, then either the two different tools must be able to use each other's native formats or a multivendor *interchange format* must be used.

The *Standard Generalized Markup Language* (SGML) is a language for logical document structure and is an international standard for publishing [66]. SGML uses the generic markup of the structural elements of a document without regard to their presentation, which is regarded as a separate issue. The *Hypermedia/Time-based Document Structuring Language* [67] (HyTime) is a standard markup language for representing hypermedia in terms of its logical structure. Its purpose is to make hypermedia interpretable and maintainable over the long term [88]. HyTime can be viewed as an application of SGML. It uses SGML syntax with its own semantics. HyTime provides standardized means of expressing information which is difficult to represent in SGML, such as the scheduling of multimedia objects in 'various coordinate spaces'.

3.7.2   Converters

The lack of agreement as to which standards or formats are best poses a dilemma for users of hypermedia. One approach to this problem relies on *converters*. Several document processing tools, such as Microsoft Word, are good at converting various image formats into a form which Microsoft Word can display.

The value of being able to exchange documents among word processing applications has led Microsoft to move in the direction of providing more compatibility between Microsoft Word and *SGML.* WordPerfect is capable of exporting and importing documents with SGML markup. One of the prominent features of the Interleaf document processing system is its ability to handle SGML logical markup.

Standards and conversions can go hand-in-hand. Converters can go from a nonstandard to a standard format or from a standard to a nonstandard format. Given n formats, about 'n times n' converters would be needed to allow a person using any format i to convert to any other format j. By using one standard as an *intermediate,* then the number of converters which is needed is reduced by a factor of '1 over n'. If a converter exists between each nonstandard format and the standard format, then going from any non-standard format to any other nonstandard format can be accomplished by going first to the standard format (see Figure 3.12).

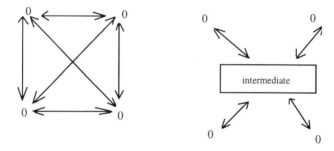

Figure 3.12: *Converters.* With 4 different end-user formats and no intermediate format, 12 converters might be needed. With an intermediate format, converters are only needed between the intermediate format and each end-user format — in this case a total of 8 converters. As the number of end-user formats increases, so does the advantage to using one intermediate format.

In the Conversion and Interchange (CI) model, every information flow needs to go through certain standard representations.

The information space is organized as the storage and within component layers of the hypermedia model. An import and export utility based on the CI submodel is attached to the *information space* (see Figure 3.13). This utility can import information from various sources in different formats to enrich the information available in the information base. On the other hand, it can export (a part of) hypermedia from the information base to a SGML document for printing or a HyTime document for interchanging with other information bases.

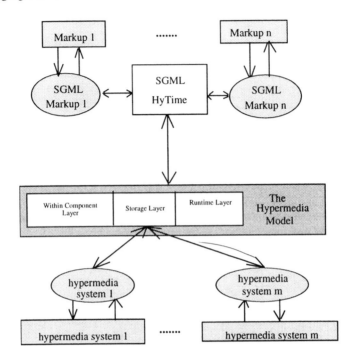

Figure 3.13: *An import and export utility.* This shows the structure of an import and export utility based on the CI model.

To support interchange, the *hypermedia system model* may be extended (see Figure 3.14). Hypermedia in the storage layer can have several instances in the runtime layer where the authoring tools work. In other words, many authors can work on the same information base simultaneously, which is the basis of local collaboration. For remote collaboration, people at different sites and/or on different platforms need to exchange information in the common information space — that is the main task of the interchange mechanism.

3.7.3   Containers

The need for converters may be remedied as well as it ever can be by new generation interchange formats, such as OpenDoc, which allow private objects and structure to be described on an equal footing with public ones. *OpenDoc* uses open, object-based, container formats. Such open object formats are combined either with platform facilities that can locate applications or with other code objects that can process a given type of data object. Thus one program can use the facilities of another program

	Runtime Layer presentation of the hypertext; user interaction; dynamics	Authoring space
The Hypermedia Model	Presentation Specification	
	Storage Layer a "database" containing a network of nodes and links	Information space
	Anchoring	
	Within Component Layer the content/structure inside the nodes	
	Interchange Mechanism	
	Communication Space	

Figure 3.14: *Groupware Model with Hypermedia Model.* In this model, an authoring space and a common information space are established on the hypermedia model.

to process those objects that it does not handle itself. Thus, someone using a word processor can incorporate in a document a spreadsheet prepared in another package which can communicate via OpenDoc with the word processor. Whenever someone wants to edit the spreadsheet, the spreadsheet program is invoked without terminating the word processing application. Of course, the user must have a copy of the spreadsheet program.

For the open container format approach to work, both the calling and responding programs — in this example a word processor and a spreadsheet — need to have a common vocabulary that defines the *embedable data objects* and how they relate to active objects (and especially to the methods on those objects.) By agreeing on a fixed, common vocabulary of methods, the application may treat the responding program as a black box and need not know details of its implementation. The degree of cooperation between the two depends on the complexity of the methods. For example, rendering a graphical object into a fixed frame is simpler than interacting with an object by selecting a portion of a display.

If the industry could agree on one standard format and consistently use it, then products could be created and distributed more easily. But this would involve some agreement among competing interests. Such agreements are not easy to achieve in rapidly evolving fields such as hypermedia. Abilities to convert from one format to another or to handle objects in open container formats will be crucial to the *dissemination* of hypermedia courseware.

3.8   Conclusion

The costs of developing courseware are great. Collecting basic materials, such as images and sound, to use in the courseware is itself an expensive operation. The challenges of overall courseware architecture are yet more demanding. Why should these efforts start anew each time? Might one *reuse* existing multimedia materials or even existing courseware in the development of new courseware?

The *Reuse Management* idiom describes a cyclic pattern of activity addressing the establishment and continual improvement of reuse-oriented activities within an organization by emphasixing learning as an institutional mechanism for change. Learning in this context means actively evaluating and reflecting on behavir to effect positive change. The *Reuse Engineering* idiom explicitly recognizes the role of the broker as a mediator between asset producers and consumers. The Reuse Management and Reuse Engineering idioms together represent reuse-specific adaptations of more general forms of organizational activity. The Framework specializes these moregeneral idioms to facilitate adaptation of a wide body of management and organizational theory to the information reuse problem.

In order for reuse to play a major part in an organization, significant time and labor must be spent on building reusable libraries. The development of such a library is a major task in and of itself. The requirements, design, implementation, testing, and maintenance of the library is necessary, and methodologies and protocols by which the library should be updated need to be established. Additionally, quality assurance standards regarding indexing of reusable components must be determined.

Courseware is a kind of *software.* The importance of reuse has been long appreciated in software engineering. The difficulty is that before the benefits of reuse can be realized, significant investment must be made in building libraries of reusable components. Numerous corporate, national, and international efforts are underway to create software reuse libraries.

A courseware reuse system should facilitate the identification of existing components that are candidates for reuse. The courseware author provides some form of component description, and the library system returns a collection of components. The author then needs to decide whether to incorporate the components into the new courseware. An overall model of the reuse process must capture the methods by which (a) an institution collects and organizes material in the reuse library, (b) users retrieve material from the library, and (c) users reorganize the material to form a coherent course.

One of the problems that frequently plagues courseware developers is the relative incompatibility of various multimedia formats. For instance, one author draws an image with one software tool and passes it to a coauthor whose authoring package does not accept images in the format tjat the first author provided. This dilemma is compounded as the courseware component gets more complicated and involves, for instance, several media or programming languages. Converters have been developed to help solve these format compatibility problems.

In assessing the costs of building a reuse library, one must not forget the costs of obtaining permission to copy someone else's material. Building a library from someone else's components entails getting the permission of the component copyright owners. Laws of *copyright* are complex and not yet well established for the areas of hypermedia or courseware.

Part II: Examples

The fundamentals of educational hypermedia, coordination, and reuse have been presented. To appreciate the practical importance of these fundamentals, the reader needs to understand what has happened in practice. To this end this Examples Part of the book details experiences with developing courseware. The two chapters in this part have been divided into a University Examples chapter and a *Commercial Examples* chapter. The methods of courseware development in universities are interestingly and importantly different from the methods in industry.

4
University Examples

Universities are facing a number of *changes* which must impact on teaching. In many places an increase in student numbers but not resources is expected [141]. The shift in emphasis is towards more student-centered learning, more distance learning, and more sharing of core course materials within and between institutions [129][133].

This chapter examines the development of courseware at universities through several *case studies*. As courseware development is a new enterprise, there are many cottage forms of it — namely, small numbers of people sometimes just one or two, who decide that they would like to experiment with the technology and demonstrate that it can be effectively used within a particular context. Some universities have, however, witnessed large, multiyear, multiperson courseware development projects, and the lessons from those projects will be emphasized here.

4.1   University of Liverpool

Many departments at the University of Liverpool are using courseware and some are involved in developing courseware. For example, the Geography Department is developing courseware as part of a consortium of three British Geography Departments, and the Latin American Studies Department has a research project concerned with developing an interactive multimedia package for a Third-Year course.

The Geography Department is developing courseware for First-Year students. The largest class sizes are in the First-Year courses, the year in which there is also the greatest conformity of course content across the different institutions. Various exercises have been written by lecturers and research students and stored on computer in the form of an online library.

The University of Liverpool English Language Unit is responsible for teaching English for academic purposes to students from overseas. The Unit is examining ways of delivering certain aspects of the courses, such as grammar practice, via computer-based, self-study packages.

The Computers in Teaching Initiative (CTI) was started by the British government to increase the effective use of educational technology, particularly computers, across the United Kingdom. Centers for each discipline were created that would promote the production and dissemination of courseware. The University of Liverpool was fortunate to have two CTI Centers.

The lecturer who directs the *CTI Center for Biology,* based at Liverpool University, believes that although high student usage is a crucial factor it does not necessarily mean that a particular course has to have high student numbers to justify use of courseware (see Figure 4.1). Lecturers in other departments and institutions in Higher Education may be interested in using, customizing, and reusing existing courseware, but they have to know that it exists in the first place. The CTI Center offers some help in this area by collecting, collating, and disseminating information about courseware. The important considerations are that courseware must be easy to obtain, easy to customize, and easy to use.

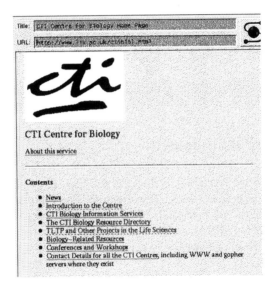

Figure 4.1: *CTI Biology Home Page:* This window shows the World Wide Web home page of the CTI Center for Biology that is located at the University of Liverpool.

The *CTI Center for Chemistry* was set up in 1989 at the University of Liverpool. The Center's original goal was to promote the use of computers in the teaching of chemistry at the higher education level. The Center considers that this does not accurately reflect the nature of the service that it currently provides nor wishes to provide in the future. The Center has thus amended its mission statement to reflect its current and future activity: to enhance the quality of teaching and learning through the use of appropriate educational technology. Of the many services offered by the CTI Center for Chemistry is a vast catalogue of courseware for chemistry (see Figure 4.2).

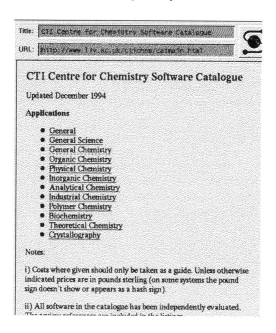

Figure 4.2: *CTI Center Catalogue*: This window from the World Wide Web onto the CTI Center for Chemistry catalogue shows the long list of chemistry topics that is covered by the catalogue.

The Department of Latin American Studies provides a rationale for the use of courseware quite different from the ones so far discussed. Work here does not involve high student usage; rather, it has the characteristics of a research project. Forty hours of documentary film were collected and then painstakingly distilled into 30 minutes of material for the courseware itself. The development of the interface to the video and the types of interaction to control were developed as the video and audio — which ethnographic studies had provided — were assessed. The two developers of the Latin American Studies courseware worked closely together. Each was committed to the effort and put many unpaid hours into the work. Contacts were maintained with other experts, but the bulk of the work regularly fell on the shoulders of the two primary people. Although one person was defined as the leader and the evaluator, both shared these and the other functionalities. It is difficult to cost this development process, and so, there is little mechanism by which the budget to develop a similar piece of courseware could be estimated.

4.2   MIT's Athena Project

The Massachusetts Institute of Technology (MIT) Athena Project was set up in the early 1980s to examine diverse uses of computing in a university (see Figure 4.3). It included educational, technical, and organizational aspects and was intended to explore the following questions:

*   What does it take to design, implement, and operate a fully distributed computing environment for a university?
*   How do students and staff use such an environment?
*   Who should maintain and manage the environment?

Virtually all undergraduates use the system and so do many others at the university. Athena has over 600 publicly accessible workstations that students and faculty can access 24 hours a day, 365 days a year.

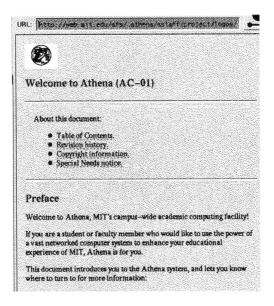

Figure 4.3: *Athena Home Page:*   This window on the WWW site http://web.mit.edu/afs/.athena/astaff/project/logos/olh/welcome shows the introduction to the Athena system.

The *Athena Project* had successes and failures. Some of the latter were due to the experimental nature of the project itself. During the first stages of Athena, it was claimed that too much time and effort were needed to build courseware because no authoring system or development tools existed. It was important that courseware production should be cost-effective. Consequently in the mid-1980s the Athena project built its own courseware authoring environment called *AthenaMuse*.

The Athena environment initially relied on several expensive hardware platforms and a single operating system. Next Athena moved from the idea of hardware and operating system coherence to that of data and application coherence. This refers to the interchange of data among computers and utilizes services such as electronic mail and online course catalogues. Thus people can use commercial software in the hardware and operating system of their choice and easily access common services.

Athena began with concerns for usability but then spent the major part of its early years dealing with *technical challenges.* In the early years of the Athena Project the systems and services changed rapidly. This led to the perception among users that the project was unstable and unreliable. Although this situation was rectified and the stability of the project secured, the earlier negative belief was not possible to completely counteract. This was a problem of adaptability caused mainly by the transition from mainframe to distributed computing and incompatibilities between the various systems involved.

4.2.1 Physical Geography Tutor

The *Physical Geography Tutor* courseware was developed using Athena software and is a preparatory guide to students in the area of engineering geology. The Tutor contains 250 short text documents and 500 photographic images that describe various geological features. All information is indexed and cross referenced through hypertext ties. This allows students to use a table of contents and an index as conventional entry points. Navigation can be in the form of selecting 'hotwords' and following the link to view a reference by using a 'lookup' capability, which includes the functions of both a table of contents and an index.

The Tutor courseware developers feel offers more to the students than conventional methods of delivery. Tutor allows students to work through a set of example case histories and then add their own to the list. In this way the Tutor can become a *personalized experience base* which can expand as the student proceeds through his or her studies or professional career.

As in many other Athena-funded projects, students were encouraged to become active in the courseware construction process. During the semester, undergraduates worked an average of 10 hours per week on the project, mainly entering text and quiz questions. Therefore, the *students* were not only users but also *developers.* Involved in the development as they were, students were more likely to give feedback and suggest useful improvements.

Development was *team-based*. The process itself was informal with most communication being of a verbal nature. The delivery of the courseware was found to be an important motivation for continuing work. This motivation was also the basis of a close relationship between the groups responsible for Athena and the Physical Geography Tutor.

4.2.2   TUDOR

Athena at MIT included projects to provide courseware simulations. The *TUDOR* project was concerned with Fluid Mechanics. Teaching staff were interested in using the computer to provide graphics and animations to demonstrate solutions of complicated equations and motion of an invisible medium. An evaluation of the project by members of staff showed clearly that the simulations were useful. However, there was some concern that computers might usurp or threaten the traditional relationship of student and tutor or might minimize the theoretical side of the subject.

The conditions surrounding the actual construction of TUDOR had an affect on the traditional educational structures in use at MIT. Students were encouraged to produce material and modules for the project and this was seen by most as a successful method of course production. Not only does it reduce pressures on busy teaching staff, but it also ensures that the focus is directed on areas which are considered important or problematic by the students themselves. Of course academics still need to guide the students in this and not all material could be developed in this way, but the fact is that some very good TUDOR courseware was *developed by students*.

TUDOR developers used the *BLOX software package* to create dynamic and interactive problem sets. BLOX also allowed multiple work areas, menu-driven choices, and graphics. The interactive interface required little computer expertise. To minimize errors and maximize ease of use input was generally done with a mouse rather than a keyboard.

TUDOR not only had a profound effect on the role of the learner, but also on the entire faculty of a division. The whole *curriculum* was reexamined to discover ways in which computers could contribute to improvements in the communication of their discipline. Traditional topics were decomposed by both content and in light of the new technology available. For example, graphics packages were implemented in certain areas, workstations with simulation packages in others. Changes occurred because of computer use and the potential benefits it could bring.

4.2.3 Pervasive

Using workstations was found to have an effect on the wider academic community. Substantial use of electronic mail, electronic discussion groups, computer-based course work, asynchronous access to teaching staff, and online library information all helped to encourage communication and *collaboration* throughout MIT.   Many, many courseware packages have been developed through Athena at MIT.

Two pieces of general-purpose course software developed on Athena include:

- The *Networked Educational Online System* (also known as Turn-in/Pickup) allows students to turn in, and their instructors to grade and return, assignments electronically.
- *Online TA* is a system by which students in a course may consult electronically with their while logged in and working on an assignment. Among the software developed to help teach specific course material, a significant fraction use the computer as a simulator of complex systems.

Some of the many successful pieces of courseware include the following [84]:

- GrowlTiger, a program used by students designing complex structures in Civil and Mechanical Engineering;
- the Computer Aided Thermodynamics package, developed in the Department of Mechanical Engineering;
- a Cardiovascular Simulator, used in teaching a Health Sciences and Technology subject in Quantitative Physiology;
- the Graphics Makes Argument Theory Simple system used to analyze debates and arguments, developed in the Political Science Department;
- a suite of graphically-oriented software for teaching Solid State Chemistry;
- a suite of software for working in Japanese, including word processing tools, dictionaries, and the ability to send mail and read Internet newsgroups in Japanese;
- a simulation that models ground water contamination, written by faculty in Civil Engineering and since used by Chemical Engineering students to design a plan for hazardous waste cleanup;
- ray tracing software used in conjunction with AutoCAD by students in architecture design classes; and
- programs for teaching students how to think about differential equations.

Faculty have requested installation of Athena capabilities in *classrooms* so that educational software may be incorporated directly into the teaching of a subject. As of 1994 Athena had two 'electronic classrooms', each equipped with about 20 Athena workstations, and a number of MIT classrooms have been equipped with Athena projection capability. In addition to its expected effects in the classroom, Project Athena and its descendants have had substantial effects on the academic community at MIT, and on the ability and inclination of faculty and students to communicate easily and effectively.

4.3   Purdue's Escape

The Purdue University Schools of Engineering provide a massive educational program across the major engineering disciplines (see Figure 4.4). The Engineering Specific Career-planning and Problem-solving Environment (ESCAPE) was created at Purdue University for preprofessional engineering courses to offer students advice on career planning. The premise was that with the computer the students might get a more dynamic and stimulating insight into engineering than with more conventional forms of presentation.

ESCAPE allowed students to design and develop their own materials to suit their own needs. Students were encouraged to create individual *career-planning workbooks* using it. Each student was provided with a modifiable template to act as the basis of their workbook.

One of the goals of the ESCAPE project was to make education fun. To achieve this, *multimedia,* including digitized sound, color graphics and video, was employed. However, this was not an overall success as the project suffered technical difficulties that resulted in the production of less than was anticipated in this area.

Initially, *HyperCard* was thought to have the capability to represent both the engineering structure and content through databases of linked text or graphics and simulations. These functions were useful, but they were found to be too simple and therefore eventually limited the development of the project.

The issue of availability consumed a great deal of the project's time and resources. The project was intended to be used by all First-Year engineering students, but as this would put a strain on existing computing resources, it was decided to switch from the Computing Center's Macintosh computers to the Engineering School's newly acquired Sun workstations. The high-speed processing capabilities, high-resolution graphics, and large memory were advantages of moving to workstations, but increased availability was the major reason. The transfer to *workstations* required a restructuring of the entire system.

An emphasis on the role of *networks* came fairly late in this project. This resulted in the project's educational goals not really being revised to take into account any benefits afforded by student-student interaction across networks. Networks were used in a more traditional sense — to provide access to a central dataset and allow for easy

Figure 4.4: *Purdue Engineering Home Page*: This window on the Purdue Schools of Engineering home page www.ecn.purdue.edu shows the beginning of the long list of Schools within the Schools of Engineering.

access and maintenance.

4.4 Organizational Issues

A common method of courseware production is based on a *team development* approach. The reasons for the existence of a team and of its constituents varies from project to project. For instance, some can be seen as software design teams and others as courseware design teams. There are important differences between the two. Larger teams are required for developing software than for courseware.

It is important to *maintain* any product to stop it falling into disuse. This is an organizational issue. Faculty conceptualize courseware and often play a large part in its development, and they have tended to see courseware in the same way as they would a publication, that is. once it is finished and delivered that is the end of the matter. This is detrimental to the longevity of the courseware. Athena recognized this and attempted to solve the problem by having as one of its goals to help the faculty produce maintainable software and watch over it once it was created.

The two most important resources for the initial creation of courseware are human and technical, but its continuation and expansion are mainly dependent on organizational resources. Three different *organizational models* support courseware development and its processes. Each model is highly dependent on the type of organizational structure that existed during the courseware's creation. The three primary organizational models are (see Figure 4.5):

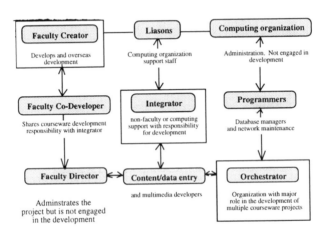

Figure 4.5: *Courseware Organization.* The creator, integrator, and orchestrator roles are depicted here.

The *creator organization* is the traditional academic structure for course design and implementation. An individual faculty member takes on the responsibility for both administration and creation. Where faculty created courseware, there was an emphasis on the need for technical resources that would allow a great deal of adaptability. This type of structure is dependent on the enthusiasm and talents of one person.

The *integrator organization* is characterized by the role of the integrator. This refers to an individual who is engaged in a partnership with the faculty. The integrator had responsibility for development but was neither a faculty member nor part of the main computing organization of the university.

The *orchestrator organization* is characterized by the role of a third organization to support the development of courseware. Such an organization was most likely to be used when the project was involved in creating its own software tools. The orchestrator tends to support many courseware products at one time. This is a particularly dynamic model as it allows the various roles within it to change and grow. Within this model the role of integrator still exits. A mutually beneficial relationship is created by using the strengths of the departmentally based projects to provide the content and part of the human resources, whereas the orchestrator provides support in the form of technical resources and advice.

There is perhaps another organizational model, called the learner construction organization in which students author courseware. The issues of limited time and skills that are prominent problems in faculty-based development are often missing from student-based development. Student-based development also brings benefits to the student. The student gains greater motivation for his or her course, as well as improved cognitive skills.

4.5   Conclusion

Universities are major users of and developers of courseware. In this chapter several *case studies* are presented of the development of courseware at universities. The first set of case studies come from a fairly typical British university. Various Schools in the university are trying to establish ways of developing teaching material in this new medium.

Massachusetts Institute of Technology (MIT) and Purdue University are major producers of courseware. The MIT effort was funded by research monies but involved the entire Institute over many years. The Purdue effort was devoted toward improving education of first-year engineers. Both the MIT and Purdue experience showed the importance of *long-term commitment* to courseware products, to maintain and distribute them — a commitment that is often not found in the developers of university courseware.

The methodology of collaborative courseware production by academics is not as advanced as the methodology of software engineering, even though the final product may be very similar. This is partly explained by academic courseware designers and authors conceiving the production of course materials as an *artistic endeavor,* as opposed to a manufacturing process. It is also to a fair degree because there can be fewer objective tests as to both the completeness and the quality of the courseware.

Three contexts exert an influence on educational computing and its success or failure:

* the *educational context,*
* the *technical context,* and
* the *organizational context.*

A well-established link between the courseware developers and a computing organization (internal or external to the institution) seems to enhance the chances of a successful project. It is important to balance the educational and technical considerations within the organizational structure.

With advances in modern computing techniques it is no longer necessary to have the user and the developer working on different platforms. This collaboration between the two interested parties might mean that the educational goals of the courseware would be reached more quickly. Therefore, active *learner participation* in courseware development should be encouraged.

5
Commercial Examples

The major barriers to coordination and reuse are often claimed to be managerial or organizational, in the sense of organizing people not organizing information. Profit-making *companies* address management differently than universities.

In this chapter the coordination for reuse as experienced in software reuse efforts at International Business Machines Corporation (IBM) and Hewlett-Packard Corporation are summarized. Far more software companies exist than courseware companies, but a number of successful courseware development companies have been established. For this chapter two courseware companies, FutureMedia and AMTECH, were investigated with a view toward establishing their requirements for a courseware development system. Investigated are not only the main processes involved in courseware development, but also the communications requirements among authors and the facilities they require to perform their designated tasks effectively.

5.1   IBM

Most major companies have quality management programs. IBM's quality management approach has as a major element the increased reuse of valuable assets to prevent redundant development and maintenance efforts. In the late 1980s, IBM launched a *worldwide campaign* to implement reuse formally into the processes of its internal operations.

Significant accomplishments have been made within IBM since the early 1980s in reuse technology. Sites such as Boblingen, Germany, Houston, Texas, and Poughkeepsie, New York have participated in this work. Part of the effort to formalise the management of reuse in IBM can be traced to the work in Boblingen on building blocks. Subsequently the *IBM Corporate Reuse Council* was established. The Council established broad communication channels. These took many forms, including newsletters, a 'starter kit', and electronic bulletin boards [140].

A focal group called the Reuse Technology Support Center was formed in January 1991. Its responsibility was to coordinate the reuse effort within IBM, provide consulting to technical organizations, and provide funds for tools and assets. In addition, reusable parts technology centers were established. As writing reusable software costs more initially than other software, *management support* is needed to make that investment possible.

The application of reuse at IBM was recognized to occur at different levels. The implementation of reuse in a business area entails exploiting opportunities for reuse across multiple contracts or products. For project-level reuse the key activity is the establishment of a *project reuse team leader*. The leader participates in all of the project reviews and must be aware of external sources for reusable components.

Implementing reuse for a site requires additional *coordination*. A site champion is given broad coordination responsibilities. A common library of reusable parts is established. The primary focus of the IBM reuse program is to establish reuse across an entire site. Different sites within IBM have taken different approaches to populating their reuse libraries. Some examine their current development efforts and identify and build reuse candidates, whereas other sites solicit donations.

When the *IBM Reuse Technology Center* was formed, it targeted five sites for support during the first year. By 1993, 30 sites worldwide were involved with the Center. The best programs showed savings in the millions of dollars and reuse accounted for 25% of the components in a software product. There have been cases where the finely tuned data abstractions provided by the building blocks exhibited better performance characteristics than custom-built data structures. These projects have benefited from the reduced maintenance costs as well as the improved performance gains.

Few major breakthroughs are necessary to exploit reuse. Certain attributes of software make software easier to reuse, but these are not necessary for reuse. IBM experience shows that reuse can be accomplished successfully in existing products with *existing techniques and knowledge*.

At the IBM system software development site in Boblingen, Germany, the first reusable parts center was established in 1987. The objective of the parts center is the production of highly generic reusable software components for worldwide use within IBM [146]. The Bobligen approach followed 5 steps: (a) define the goal, (b) determine critical success factors, (c) define required activities, (d) validate plan, and (e) execute activities. The goal was to establish a well-defined reuse program within 2 years that would shorten development time, increase reliability of products, and increase the extent of reuse. Brainstorming contributed to the determination of *critical success factors*.

The IBM reuse goal was seen to have aspects of trading. In other words, for assets to have multiple applications, it is necessary to establish a trading infrastructure to link customers and suppliers. The elements of a *marketplace* are derived from the fact that suppliers offer parts and customers require parts.

To store and advertise the parts to be traded, a repository for holding the parts as well as their description is needed. *Traders* must also trust the quality of the parts. As quality is often loosely interpreted, IBM preferred to use the concept of certification level. This means a guaranteed completeness and defect rate of a part. Additionally, the purchaser of a part wants some maintenance assurances. Some kind of accounting is required to record exchanges and associated costs and savings.

Overall, the determination of critical success factors identified the following factors: motivation, education, requirements for parts, offering of parts, part library, quality criteria, maintenance, progress control, and accounting. To increase *motivation*, incentives were introduced as an activity. A part library could initially be a simple list, but communication channels are needed to make known and accessible this library. As the library grows, structured methods and tools to support the library are needed. For certification levels, the lowest was 'as-is' for software that was not designed to be reusable but might be of use to someone. The medium level certification indicated a part that can be reused without additional explanation. Maintenance changes to software must be accommodated by the library. *Education* is important at IBM and an appropriate curriculum addressing all aspects of reuse was created.

Two extreme modes of inserting new technologies are the *grassroots* and the *edict* approaches. IBM used both. Edicts quickly generate some results. However, experience showed that acceptance by staff of the methodology is not necessarily obtained by the edict approach. Grassroots projects requires patience on behalf of the funding bodies. Although incentives are inexpensive, IBM experience showed that only people who already have some affinity to a method will be further motivated by incentives.

The constraints of development organizations to deliver products to market in the shortest possible time does not allow room for additional efforts to produce generalized software. The production of building blocks is therefore the responsibility of parts centers. The scope of the *parts center* may be of various types. At IBM Boblingen the library is of the horizontal type and provides general-purpose building blocks usable in almost any application, such as queues. A vertical type of library was developed and maintained at IBM in Rockville, Maryland. The vertical approach requires that parts be available which are of higher abstraction than needed for the next product release.

At IBM Boblingen the first step in technology transfer was to teach and distribute information about reuse methodology and parts. This step did not actually lead to the application of the new methods. A second step of advice and consultation was added. The decision to get reusable parts for product development happens during the design phase. Therefore consultation was offered to projects in the design phase. This offer was welcomed but not really used. In many projects, design happens very informally and interactively and consultation does not readily fit into this mode of work. Thus IBM introduced a third step, called *fingertip reuse* into the technology transfer process (see Figure 5.1). Fingertip reuse includes the availability of a tool with which a designer can look for reusable parts within seconds, just when it comes to mind. Otherwise, the threshold of asking for consultation proved too high.

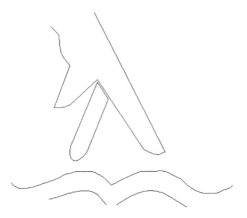

Figure 5.1: *Fingertip Reuse.* The figure shows two fingers walking across a book.

The metaphor of 'let your fingertips do the walking' that has been popularised through advertising for *Yellow Pages* is appropriate to software reuse. The Yellow Pages are accessible within moments at most offices and homes and users know how to instantly find something that would otherwise be time-consuming to find.

As a result of its efforts in reuse, IBM Boblingen was able to triple its reuse rate within 12 months. However, increasing financial and administrative independence of company divisions may lessen opportunities for reuse. The application of the Critical Success Factors method helped the planning and implementing of a reuse strategy, but the execution of the activities required *iterative readjustment.*

5.2   HP

Hewlett-Packard (HP) has been engaged in reuse since the early 1980s [48]. At the end of the 1980s HP established a corporate-wide reuse strategy. This lead in the early 1990s to the successful application of reuse on a larger scale and the development of further reuse libraries.

The HP *corporate reuse strategy* involves a core team of reuse experts with additional people working on assignments with several HP pilot projects. HP is divided into several large divisions, such as the printer division, and unlike some corporations, HP is not building a single corporate-wide reuse library. Rather, each division creates reuse programs and products customized to their needs. It works with the different divisions to help them exploit reuse. The core team develops economic models, coding guidelines, educational handbooks, and generally consults with the divisions. The core team focuses on domain-specific approaches to software reuse and has developed a domain analysis methodology for HP.

A study of reuse practice at HP has made it strikingly clear that the impediments to improving software reuse are predominantly nontechnical and socioeconomic. When confronted with their first reuse failure, a division should pursue an incremental improvement process. For a reuse program to be effective, the specific inhibitors likely to affect it must be identified. To better visualize these *inhibitors,* HP divides these factors into the following categories:

- people factors include culture, motivation, management, training, and skills,
- process factors include domain, economics, and standards, and
- technology factors include tools and languages.

Once the inhibitors are identified, solutions can be tried.

The most effective reuse programs concentrate on the identification and development of a small, high-quality set of needed, useful components, and make sure that the users of those components know about them. This *small library* of less than 100 components can be handled largely on paper in terms of the catalog and the distribution of information about it. Large libraries of poor-quality components with complex library system interfaces are not wanted. In this way, significant levels of reuse can be achieved in any language with very little tool support. From this base, the reuse effort can grow.

In 1992 HP Laboratories (the research division of HP) initiated a comprehensive, multidisciplinary reuse program. Although the library metaphor has guided much work, HP Laboratories is exploring an alternative metaphor to the library. Typically, in the library-centered reuse approach, software code libraries are intended to attract users who have a system design and want a tailorable part. The HP Laboratory metaphor is called domain-specific kits and corresponds to the commercial children's toys from LEGO Systems, Inc., called *LEGO building blocks.* The LEGO metaphor suggests parts that fit together and exhibit ease of use. Over the years, the LEGO Systems building blocks have evolved from a small variety of simple generic parts to a rich family of kits. Kits for spacecraft, for farms, and other domains exist. Each system comes carefully packaged with instructions for how to use it and may sometimes contain frameworks, such as a space platform. The HP Laboratories approach to reuse exchanges the library metaphor with the domain-specific kit metaphor. The domain-specific kit includes components, frameworks, glue languages, generic applications, tools, environments, and processes (see Figure 5.2).

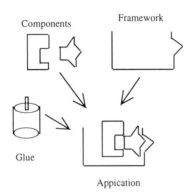

Figure 5.2: *Kit*: In the domain-specific kit, components are placed within a framework and connected with glue.

One way to design a *software factory* based on the kit approach is to consider inputs of user needs and purchased software parts into the factory (see Figure 5.3). Kit developers than take these two inputs and develop reuse kits from them. Kit users then work with the kits to develop a rich range of applications.

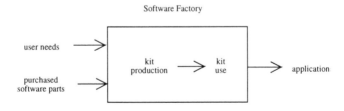

Figur 5.3: *Kit Factory*: The two inputs on the left go through kit production and kit use inside the factory before applications result.

5.3   FutureMedia

FutureMedia Limited produces hypermedia courseware for distribution on CD-ROM. Typical customers are industrial companies that wish to improve the distribution of training materials about their products. Each contract is treated as a separate project, and staff with the necessary skills are deployed to each project under the coordination of the *Project Manager,* who obtains further resources as necessary. The computer plays little part in the management process, which is undertaken using traditional tools.

At FutureMedia initial analysis revolves around the production of a script, which will later drive the design process. This script is written by the Instructional Designer in conjunction with subject specialists in the client organization. The *Instructional Designer* attempts to make the most effective use of the available technologies to deliver the training objectives, as identified by the client. The *script* describes:

- the aims of the courseware,
- the instructional strategy to be followed, and
- what will be taught to the students.

The script also estimates the length and complexity of the training material. The project team formally reviews the script with the client to determine whether it meets the client's requirements. Also, choices must be discussed that involve considerable differences in cost.

Once the script has been agreed, the next stage is to turn it into a series of *storyboards,* which show in detail what is required in each module. In particular, the media to be used will be decided at this stage. This is so that the most appropriate project team may be assembled to actually write the final courseware.

A team of experts can then be assembled to participate in the detailed design of the courseware. This *team* will include numerous roles, each of which may or may not be performed by one person. Three sample roles are:

- Graphic Designer who will develop graphics and animation;
- Video producer who will take charge of the production of quality video images which will conform exactly to the script;
- Software designer who will control the way the media hangs together.

Generally the team produce and discuss ideas, reacting to those ideas by agreeing or disagreeing with their content, and finally agree to a presentation that will be taken to the client. If the client disagrees with the proposed design, then the designers either defend their case or, more likely, attempt to modify the design to meet the client's needs. The final result is a script for the final production, which must be approved by the *content expert*. In the design phase, the role of the team members has been to act, more or less, as consultants but in the implementation phase the collaborative aspect becomes more important. Continual communication is vital. The *instructional designer* , however, controls the overall process.

If there is a need for information thatalready exists, then a decision must be made as to whether to incorporate this rather than to create the material anew. Reuse decisions are affected by availability, time constraints, budget constraints, feasibility, suitability of previously stored information, and quality. The evaluation of the feasibility of reusing information only takes place at this implementation stage and not before. During the previous stages the idea of reuse is not considered. There is a feeling that a house style may add to the success of the company. This would support *reuse* as well as ensure good practices are followed. As yet this has not happened but may become important in the near future as the number of completed sets of courseware grows.

The methodology of the interactions between the members of the team have become well established. Projects generally last 6 months to a year. All functionalities of team members, such as team worker, leader, and evaluator are required, as well as the skill experts, such as video producer and instructional designer.

5.4   AMTECH Courseware Life Cycle

The Gruppo Agusta, an organization of about 10,000 employees, is the unique designer and manufacturer of helicopters in Italy, and one of the leading companies in the world. In order to better approach the application of new technologies to education and training, Gruppo Agusta established the new company AMTECH. AMTECH is a commercial courseware development company of 100 people. AMTECH has well defined courseware life cycle phases, each of which includes a rigorous quality control review by senior officials of AMTECH. AMTECH has successfully developed numerous computer-based training packages (see Figure 5.4).

The *courseware life-cycle* at AMTECH has six phases or activities (see Figure 5.5):

1.   requirements and planning,
2.   preliminary design,
3.   storyboard production,
4.   implementation,

5.   integration, and
6.   delivery.

All the phases are subject to *quality control* in order to establish conformity to the relevant specifications. The quality control is performed on both the result and the methodology used to generate it. Active customer involvement in the process is a must for the project success.

Topic	Traning Hours	Customer
A129 Helicopter	70	Italian Army
B412 Helicopter	34	Italian Army
EH101 Helicopter	40	Pilatus Aircraft Ltd. Switzerland
Stall	4	ALITALIA
Radar-altimeter	7	MSE
AB-INITO computer	152	Natioanl Flight School of Sweden
Sysmology	4	Regione Lombardia
English Language Learning	56	General Public

Figure 5.4: *Computer-Based Training Packages.* For courses developed by Augusta AMTECH, the first column is the topic of the courseware, the second column is the number of hours of training which the courseware provided, and the third column is the customer for the training.

Courseware product development originates from a customer training request. The customer training request is the basis for generating a development contract. Starting from the development contract, the project group:

•   identifies the training goals of the courseware and the target population;
•   defines how the training goals will be met; and
•   plans the activities needed to develop the courseware.

In the 'Requirement and Planning' phase the project group issues the *Courseware Requirements* document, which describes a hardware and software architecture; applicable teaching strategy; and interconnection between the different components of the courseware. At the same time, the *Courseware Development Plan* document is issued and describes the needed resources and the time schedule. In addition, the Courseware Test Plan document is produced and describes the testing methodology.

A *Requirements Review* is held to verify the completeness of the requirements and to approve the testing criteria. The following staff take part in the Requirements Review:

- The Didactic Systems Office Manager (President);
- The Software Project Quality Representative (Secretary);
- One or More Customer Representatives;
- The Configuration Management Representative;
- The Training Systems Technical Manager;
- The Quality Assurance Manager;
- The Project Technical Manager;
- Current Documentation Authors; and
- Other specialists according to the President's judgment.

At the end of the meeting, a report is issued that describes the problems encountered, the corrective actions to be performed, and the time necessary to complete them.

During the design phase, the customer is allowed to analyze a sample lesson that shows the training strategy and some courseware graphics, audio, and video. This phase is completed once the *Design Review* is held. The staff that take part in the Design Review are basically the same as those who take part in the Requirements Review.

For any single lesson, a storyboard is drafted on paper to describe what will be implemented on the computer in terms of:

- objects to be drawn on the screen;
- interaction with the trainee;
- text layout;
- audio sentences; and
- flow charts to describe the logical links among the blocks of frames constituting a particular topic in the section.

The *storyboards* allow the simulation of the lesson before its implementation on the computer. The Courseware Designer, with the possible help of the Subject Matter Expert, issues the storyboards of the current module, on the basis of agreed standards which are contained in the documents issued during the previous activities. The storyboards, together with the relevant flow charts, are gathered in the Storyboard Collection document.

In the *Implementation phase,* the storyboards are implemented on the computer. All the graphics, texts and logical links of the lesson are developed. At the same time, the visual and audio material is implemented in a preliminary way.

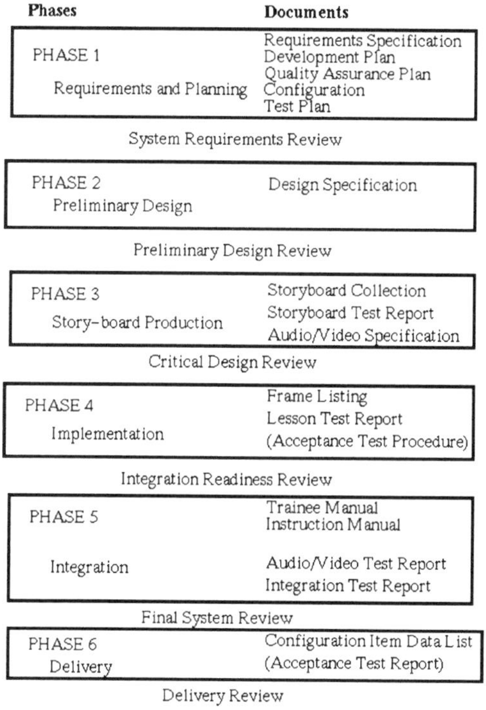

Phases	Documents
PHASE 1 Requirements and Planning	Requirements Specification Development Plan Quality Assurance Plan Configuration Test Plan

System Requirements Review

PHASE 2 Preliminary Design	Design Specification

Preliminary Design Review

PHASE 3 Story-board Production	Storyboard Collection Storyboard Test Report Audio/Video Specification

Critical Design Review

PHASE 4 Implementation	Frame Listing Lesson Test Report (Acceptance Test Procedure)

Integration Readiness Review

PHASE 5 Integration	Trainee Manual Instruction Manual Audio/Video Test Report Integration Test Report

Final System Review

PHASE 6 Delivery	Configuration Item Data List (Acceptance Test Report)

Delivery Review

Figure 5.5: *The AMTECH Courseware Life-Cycle.* The name of each of the 6 phases is given in the left-hand side of each box. The review step that occurs between each phase is indicated with the label between each pair of adjacent boxes. The documents that result from a phase are listed in the right-hand side of the box describing the phase.

In the *Integration phase,* graphics and text are integrated with the final audio and video. At the same time, the Courseware Usage Manuals are produced. Those manuals will contain an exhaustive summary of the contents in each lesson in the course. In particular the Manual for the Instructor will contain a list of all tests. A Final System Review is held to analyze and approve the issued documentation, and to examine and approve the courseware produced. In this phase, the final version of the course is officially delivered to the Customer.

The hardware and the software are guaranteed by the contract. The *Courseware Guarantee* covers any eventual technical problems. Errors have to be signaled with a document written by the Customer containing:

- complete courseware identifier;
- description of the frame where the error has occurred;
- error description; and
- description of the conditions in which the error has occurred.

The error report will be assessed by the producer in order to guarantee a quick action. Any modifications to the produced courseware involve an update of the documentation. The corrected courseware will be submitted to all the tests provided for the integration phase. The Customer can request modifications involving substantial variations to the delivered courseware, but pursuing these modifications requires a new, dedicated contract.

5.5   AMTECH Courseware

A course developed by Augusta AMTECH has a standard structure. Each course is split into modules that identify one or more *subject areas*. A subject area will cover one or more *training objectives* inside the course. Special *area tests* are scheduled to check the knowledge reached by the trainee. Inside an area test, the trainee has to pass the proposed tests. Tests are chosen randomly from the same data base and used during the lesson phase.

A *module* is split into one or more *lessons*. Each of them will describe one topic. The topic will be provided to the trainee during a teaching session. A teaching session should be 45 minutes in duration, between two teaching sessions a break has to be allowed. Recurrent parts are present in each lesson which describe contents and give general information about a lesson (see Figure 5.6). These parts are lesson title, lesson description, and lesson conclusion. The lesson title is a standard format frame containing the title of the lesson. The lesson description is a standard format frame, or a series of frames, stating:

- lesson objective;
- what the trainee will be able to achieve at the end of the lesson;
- prerequisite background necessary to reach the lesson; and

- lesson length.

The lesson conclusion is a standard format frame that reports general information when the trainee has completed the lesson and includes lesson leaving message and next lesson to perform.

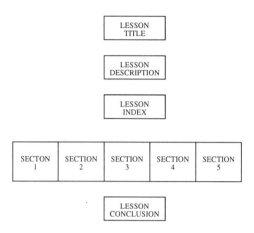

Figure 5.6: *Lesson Structure.* Describes the contents of each lesson and gives information about the lesson.

A *lesson* is split into sections. The maximum number of sections in a lesson is five. The lesson index presents exclusively the section names. Each section is split into four distinct and consecutive teaching parts:

- introduction
- presentation
- review
- test

The introduction allows the trainee to evaluate whether he is already confident with the section subject. Having seen this the trainee may elect to skip to the review or test phase.

The *lesson index* is a standard format frame that allows the trainee to make active a section. To select a section, the trainee has to touch the section name on the touch screen. If a not-permitted selection is made, nothing happens.

Command bars allow the trainee to perform some choices inside the lesson. There are three command bars used in the lesson structure:

- *main command bar:* allows the trainee to move inside the lesson following the logical path from the beginning (introduction phase of the first section) to the end (test phase of the last section);
- *choice command bar:* allows the trainee to reach any part of the lesson if allowed;
- *utilities command bar:* allows the trainee to achieve some options useful during lesson delivery,such as to turn off the audio, to get help, or to exit.

The following general rules apply to the command bars:

- the command bars will always appear at the bottom of the screen;
- the command bars will switch on only the options selectable by the trainee in that moment;
- each option in the command bars will be symbolized by a graphic icon representative of its function;
- the icon position inside each command bar will be logical and easy to remember (e.g., to go forward at the bottom right corner of the screen to go back at the left corner);
- the common icons between different command bars will have the same position;
- the help option will always be present;
- an option of the command bars is made active by touching it (no more is asked).

These kinds of design rules, although in some ways obvious, serve to guide the courseware developers and to insure a uniform and high-quality product.

The AMTECH training system is controlled by main *computers* that manage the trainee stations in the classroom. Each classroom is equipped with an instructor station and a large screen system connected to the instructor station. Both the trainee station and the instructor station are color videographics terminals with audio capabilities.

5.6   Conclusion

The construction of domain models and libraries that support *reuse* has occurred in numerous organizations. The costs of developing and maintaining the libraries are high and only systematic, reuse-oriented management of the staff leads to long-term benefits exceeding cost. This chapter has documented experiences of reuse at IBM and HP.

At IBM, *fingertip reuse* has proved critical to user acceptance. If engineers must consult with the corporate or division reuse librarians in formalized ways, the engineers will not bother to follow the reuse plan. With fingertip reuse, a designer can look for reusable parts within seconds, just when it comes to mind.

The HP experience is consistent with that of IBM. HP found that the most effective reuse programs concentrate on a small, high-quality set of useful components, and make sure that the engineers know about this small library. Careful focused management of *incremental change* is the key to reuse.

The experiences of software development companies are germane to the work of *courseware development companies.* Of the many courseware companies that develop training material for the commercial sector, some are small and independent and serve many different customers, but others are intimately connected to a large corporation whose needs for training material the courseware company exclusively provides. The small company, FutureMedia, is an independent company with diverse customers, and the company, Agusta AMTECH, is a company within a company that develops courseware targeted to its parent company.

FutureMedia assigns a *project leader* to each contract which FutureMedia has for a courseware product. This project leader must liaise closely with the customer and with specialists within FutureMedia to assure that a product is cost-effectively produced that satisfies the customer. The guidelines for the execution of a project are not rigorously defined, and a project leader is largely free to adopt whatever method of courseware development seems most suited to the case at hand.

The procedures at Agusta AMTECH, on the other hand, are rigorously defined. Courseware project procedures are controlled by the courseware life cycle, which has six phases: requirements, design, storyboard production, implementation, integration, and delivery. Precisely defined hardware and software delivery platforms constrain how the lesson can be taught. Perhaps this regimented approach to courseware development is partially a reflection of the close connection of AMTECH to its massive, parent firm Agusta and the well-established policies of Agusta. Perhaps the organization-wide policies of AMTECH, which apply consistently to all courseware products developed at AMTECH, are partially a reflection of the relatively homogeneous customer needs. Whatever the reason, the procedures at AMTECH are impressive for their uniformity and for their reflection of a *manufacturing approach* to the development of courseware.

As more teaching materials are produced within a hypermedia framework, the possibilities for reuse expand. At AMTECH the current requirement for reuse is the ability for authors and designers to identify primitive components (pictures, diagrams, and sections of text) that they wish to reuse and to be able to convert them from one format to another. However, libraries of reusable courseware material do not exist at either AMTECH or FutureMedia. Both companies anticipate a time when the creation and maintenance of reuse libraries will prove cost-effective, and AMTECH is actively investing in the development of tools and methods for the support of reusable courseware libraries.

The differences between the methods of the commercial and the academic courseware development groups are interesting. One conclusion to be drawn from the contrast between the *academic* and the commercial cases is that the characters of both the product and the people affect the mode of work. This is not a surprising conclusion in itself, but the degree to which the work styles and phases vary is most remarkable. The professional training company AMTECH with its manufacturing customers followed the classic life cycle and had specialized people in all of the critical roles of hypermedia courseware authoring. The academics, such as at the University of Liverpool and MIT, developed material in a less structured way, as they were often learning which material they wanted to convey through the experience of trying to create material. The academics did not have as clearly defined roles for the team members nor as well developed a script, as the commercial people.

Part III: Systems

Tools for the support of courseware development can improve the efficiency and effectiveness of courseware production teams. Of course, the tools must be carefully selected to fit into the workflow of those who are supposed to use the tools. This part of the book describes some systems that have been built and gives some experiences with the use of the systems. The emphasis is on the architectural features of the systems that have been built to support the coordination of authors and the reuse of educational hypermedia.

6
University Systems

At universities new tools are being developed to support the development of courseware. One example of a suite of such tools is incorporated in the *Many Using and Creating Hypermedia* (MUCH) system. The group which developed and used the MUCH system, naturally enough called the MUCH group, has been developing and delivering innovative courseware with the help of the MUCH system for many years. The system has been used in writing several hypertext books and CD-ROM products and in teaching numerous classes in special interactive ways [110]. The MUCH group is not necessarily a typical university example of a courseware development team. However the tools and methods of the MUCH group highlight how coordination and reuse can be exploited in a university environment.

The *World Wide Web* (WWW) contains a vast library of hypermedia and is used world-wide. The university experience is that student involvement in courseware authoring and team work are both valuable in successfully making educational hypermedia. Accordingly, a methodology and system have been developed, and will in the second half of this chapter be described, for collecting information from the WWW and repackaging it as cohesive, fast-access, educational hypermedia.

6.1   MUCH System Architecture

Early versions of the MUCH system used various software and hardware platforms, such as a relational database management system on mainframe computers and HyperCard on Macintoshes [107]. The version to be described in this chapter is based on networked Unix workstations and has its own unique database system. The *MUCH group* operates within a Department of Computer Science that has access to large amounts of computer equipment. Every member of the MUCH group and every student in a course can be expected to have access anytime to a powerful, graphics workstation.

6.1.1   Database

The MUCH system manages a hypermedia information database and provides facilities to support courseware publishing activities (see Figure 6.1). In the development of the MUCH environment, an object-oriented approach was adopted. The *Andrew Toolkit* (see Chapter 1) provides objects for multimedia document preparation and communication, such as objects for text, equations, spreadsheets, figures, animations, and messages. The MUCH system incorporates these Andrew objects. Utilities were developed with the Andrew Toolkit to provide services for various activities, such as collaborative authoring, management, hypermedia publishing, and document interchange.

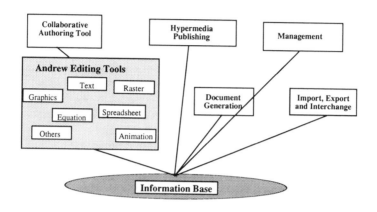

Figure 6.1: *MUCH Environment Architecture.* The central components are the information base and the Andrew editing tools.

The MUCH system design is based on the *Dexter model* (see Chapter 1). A network of nodes and links is defined in a storage layer. A within-component layer contains the actual media content to which nodes point.

The links and nodes form semantic net. A document can be generated by traversing the semantic net following a certain strategy [108]. A document is actually only nodes' contents connected together with links of certain type(s). The user can specify which type(s) of link the traversal program will follow. For example, one can generate a document with or without annotations by selecting or deselecting the annotation link types for the *traversal program* from a dialog box (see Figure 6.2). One can also choose any start node in order to generate a part of the database. The depth of the document can be specified, and the traversal program will not go deeper than this depth.

The MUCH system supports *coordination* in various ways. The MUCH mail facility is used to notify a user when someone else has made an update that overwrites the ongoing update of the user. Users are divided into two types of managers and others. Only managers can arbitrarily delete information. Others can only suggest to delete links or nodes and then await either approval from the manager or supporting statements from others.

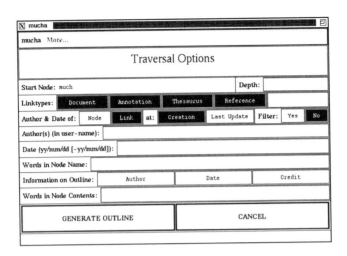

Figure 6.2: *Traversal Dialog Box.* With the traversal option dialog box the user specifies features of the traversal which the MUCH system will execute.

6.1.2   Interface

The MUCH interface was built with the Andrew Toolkit [15]. The Andrew Toolkit allows users to edit text, equations, graphs, tables, pictures, and so forth, all in a single program. Working on the content window of MUCH is just like working in Andrew's multimedia editor (see Figure 6.3), except that the edited material is a node in the MUCH information base. To add a new link, the user describes attributes of the link through a dialog box (see Figure 6.5).

When the MUCH system is started, the hypermedia information is presented on two separate windows with *fold-unfold outline* in one window and the content of a selected node in another. When the user selects a node in the fold-unfold outline, the associated content appears in the content window (see Figure 6.4). Although on the interface the logical network is presented as a tree, the data in the logical network is truly an unrestricted network rather than a tree. The outline on the hierarchical browser (outline window) is only a specific view of (a part of) the logical network. To enable users to follow the links which are not shown in the outline, a network browser is provided (see Figure 6.4).

To help users find topics of interest the MUCH system provides a word index window on which all words in the database are listed. Once a word is selected, the occurrences of the selected word are shown on the outline window as a number in front of the node including that word (see Figure 6.6). In fact, the occurrence number appears at not

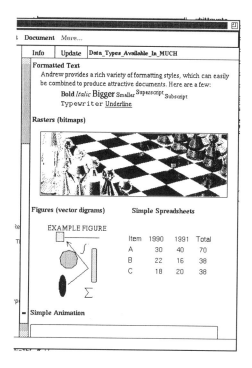

Figure 6.3: *Andrew Inset.* An example of content window that includes various insets.

only the node including the selected word but also its ancestors in order that one can easily find the node of interest when it is folded under a high level node. However, the number shown at the ancestor node is the occurrences in the whole subtree. This fold-unfold view of word distribution has proven valuable in searching tasks [35].

6.2   MUCH System Applications

The MUCH system has been used by over 300 people through a 7-year period. Applications have included the collaborative authoring of hypertext textbooks, collaborative learning in classrooms, and management of a research organization. The methods and facilities employed in these *applications* are indicative of those which would be useful in other environments for the development of educational hypermedia through the coordination of people and the reuse of hypermedia.

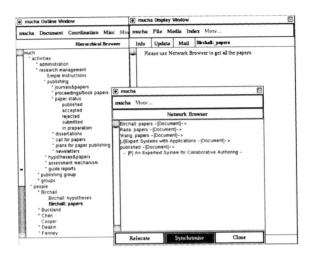

Figure 6.4: *MUCH Window.* The interface of the MUCH collaborative authoring system. The asterisks before nodes indicate that these nodes can be unfolded. The network browser window shows all the links from the highlighted node.

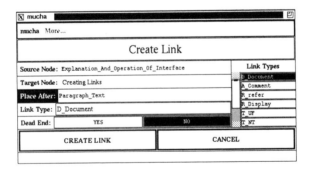

Figure 6.5: *Creating a Link.* The user has selected the node 'Explanation And Operation of Interface' and then typed 'Creating Links;', the user then decides to place the new node after 'Paragraph Text'. To confirm the link the user clicks on 'Create Link'.

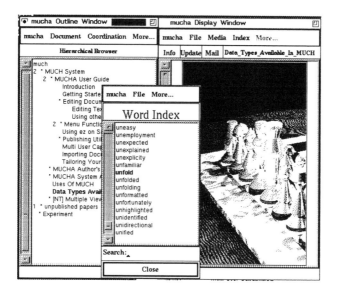

Figure 6.6: *Word Index.* Word index utility in the MUCH system to help users find information. Once a word is selected, the occurrences of the selected word are shown on the outline window as a number in front of the node including that word.

6.2.1 Writing Hypertext

The MUCH system has been repeatedly used for the *coauthoring* of teaching material. This collaboration has taken many forms, from each author being solely responsible for their individual chapters, to a division of labor in which one person collects material, another does the writing, and a third does the revising.

The participants in any collaborative endeavor need to establish ground rules to guide the collaboration. Within the MUCH authoring group it was decided to have regular weekly meetings of all the *collaborators* at which progress, problems, and ideas would be discussed. To facilitate the collaborative process, the written records of meetings were placed in the MUCH system.

One administrative problem centered around the need to establish what collaborators had done, particularly where they might have altered the work of another collaborator. When a node is created, the MUCH system records the user's identification and the time of the creation. In addition, information on all the subsequent *updates* to the node are also recorded, including user name and time (see Figure 6.7). This information can be displayed to the reader at any time.

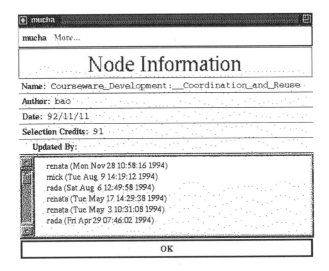

Figure 6.7: *MUCH Update.* Update information is recorded for the node 'Writing Hypertext'. Recorded information includes Author 'rada', Date '94/04/29' on which the node was created, and names and dates of who and when the node was updated.

6.2.2   Collaborative Learning

Classes have been taught with the MUCH system. This was facilitated by holding 'lectures' in a computer laboratory where students sat at computer workstations connected over a network. The course text was available online and students were encouraged to follow the text during the lectures.

After each lecture, students were asked to undertake an assignment related to the contents of the lecture. Students were assigned to teams of 3, and each *team* wrote a report. All 3 members of a team got the same grade for this part of the exercise. For another exercise, students were allocated to organizations (companies). Each organization consisted of 4 groups of 3 people. Reports of the company had to be stored in the MUCH system. Using facilities of the MUCH system, students also assessed the work of other students.

MUCH, as well as supporting collaborative work, supports *assessment.* MUCH allows users to make comments on the work of others. MUCH also records how often a particular piece of text has been selected. Each time a particular node is selected, the person who created that node is awarded a selection credit. The credit table option gives details of all of the authors and how many times each author's work has been selected (see Figure 6.8). Thus, if the assessment of a piece of work is based on how often someone views the work, MUCH has a tool to support this.

```
mucha  More...
┌──────────────────────────────────────────┐
│  Table of Authors and Select Credits      │
│   damon      (Damon Chaplin) 959          │
│   david        (David Reid)   36          │
│   hypbook     (Roy Rada et al) 126        │
│   iwc     (Dan Diaper (journal))  6       │
│   kathryn    (Miss. K.J. Coles)   1       │
│   mdb          (Martin Beer)   3          │
│   mhashi                       33         │
│   miked      (Mr. M.W. Dobson) 69         │
│   norge45     (Mr. J. Russell) 98         │
│   oscar8                        9         │
│   perena     (Miss. P.I. Gouma) 183       │
│   rada       (Prof. Roy Rada) 1266        │
│   scsr95     (Mr. P.H. Ramsey) 62         │
│   scst18     (Miss. S.A. Acquah)  7       │
│   scst49    (Mr. M.R. Anderson) 121       │
│   scst52    (Mr. A.M. Blanchard) 27       │
├──────────────────────────────────────────┤
│                  OK                        │
└──────────────────────────────────────────┘
```

Figure 6.8: *Credit Selection Table.* Users are listed in alphabetical order of their user i.d. and the frequency with which their information has been viewed is indicated in the rightmost column.

Selection credits alone are not a fair method of assessment as a very poor piece of work with an attractive node title may be selected often but actually read or appreciated very little. Also, the selection credit system is open to abuse because people can continuously select each other's work to obtain a high *selection credit total*.

One feature of the MUCH system was specifically developed for student *peer assessment*. For one student to assess another student's node content, it was necessary for the first student to read what was written in the node. An 'Assessment Window' was then used by students to help them to grade the work of their peers. Students were able to assess their colleague's work on a scale from 1 to 10, 1 being the lowest possible mark which could be awarded, and 10 being the highest. These marks were awarded based on five different criteria; namely, content, clarity, creativity, grammar and spelling (see Figure 6.9). Using this method, each student could assess the work of each of the other students in the class.

6.2.3   Management

The experience of writing courseware and of teaching classes where students worked together on the MUCH system illustrated the value of group support with the MUCH system [45]. The rapid growth of the group generated the need to induct and supervise new members. The increase in size created a need for new operational structures to maintain efficiency and productivity. The traditional communication

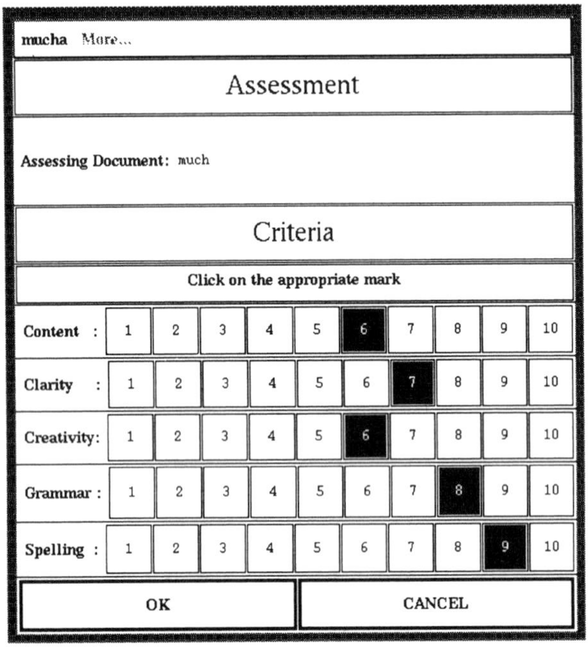

Figure 6.9: *Assessment Credit Window.* The Assessment window used to help students to grade the work of their peers. This allows students to assess the work of their peer's on a scale from 1 to 10, 1 being the lowest possible mark which could be awarded. Marks are awarded based on five different criteria.

modes (face-to-face meetings and email interaction) that had been used previously were no longer sufficient to cope with the increased group size and range of activities. The first step towards systemization was the introduction of a computer-based management support and enabling tool.

At this point in its life course the group had become an organization and had a hierarchical structure in which power was largely centralized, although some control was delegated down the organizational layers. Consistent with the ethos of a *learning organization,* it was decided at this stage that a survey should be conducted to collect data on current operations. A systematic approach was adopted to assess the needs of the group members in the light of rapid organizational change.

A questionnaire was circulated among the members of the organization. The results showed that many members were suffering from role and task *ambiguity.* Their comments were not atypical in organizations undergoing change [137]. Ambiguity forms a major source of stress. The goal to be achieved, the methods used, and the criterion by which members of an organization recognize success — any or all of these can become more ambiguous during times of change. The challenge for management is to resolve these ambiguities without simplification of the problem.

The initial response to the findings of the field study was the restructuring of the organization to take the form of a loose *matrix.* The organization was divided into groups, but group members frequently worked on different projects at the same time, reporting to one or more project managers as well as a group manager. Embodied within this new structure were formalized changes in the approach to management which attempted to address the problem of role and task ambiguity:

1. a shared group vision of short term goals was encouraged;
2. plans were developed in a manner that would engender shared responsibility;
3. evaluation of the work output was performed by checking whether the work product of each group was significant and on time.

At this point the organization could be said to have entered the *systemization phase* whereby there was greater differentiation of functions and systemization of operation. Organizations in this phase are more certain and secure. Members know where they stand and have clear guidelines about the way work should be done.

A *planning document* was drafted and entered into the MUCH system. The planning document reflected visions, objectives, strategies, and activities based on an informal 'management-by- objectives' approach. Management by objectives involves setting superordinate goals for the organization as a whole and then cascading those objectives through the organizational structure, so that goal attainment at each level helps attain goals at the next until, ultimately, the superordinate goals are attained [20]. The document was also designed to permit individual users to maintain schedules, what 'to do' notes, work diaries and progress reports (see Figure 6.10).

The introduction of the plan into the MUCH system was aimed at increasing the level of *information sharing* among group members. Each member of the organization would have access to the plan document, could identify whom to consult, and could update the plan each time a task was completed, so reducing role and task ambiguity. In addition, the supervisors (or managers) could keep track of each of their subordinate's progress by checking the updates of the document. The structure of the document further illustrates the way the plan was used (see Figure 6.11).

In order to be able to better assess the viability of the Plan Document, a statistical review of actual Plan usage was undertaken. Measurements were derived from data maintained by the MUCH system. Long term matters such as visions, plans and objectives were relatively infrequently accessed by comparison with short term matters. The tendency was to access nodes relating to visions and plans in order to become aware of and familiar with the longer term as a form of high-level reference,

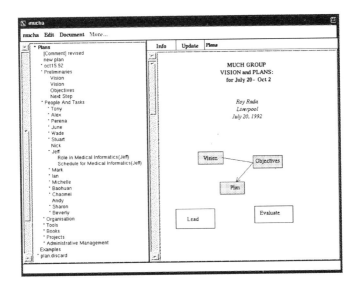

Figure 6.10: *MUCH Plan Document.* The title of the document is Plans (the top node in the tree). The outline of the document has been expanded or unfolded to show some of the nodes in the document. The level of expansion is indicated by the level of left indentation. For example, level one below Plans includes the nodes '[Comment] revised', 'new plan', 'oct 15.92', 'People And Tasks', 'Organization', and 'Administrative Management'. The People and Tasks node comprises a deep subtree as indicated by the asterisks preceding some of its subnodes. One of these has been expanded further (Jeff), and, in this case, the Jeff subtree has two nodes that are at the bottom of the subtree (leaves). The top node, Plans, is highlighted in bold text to indicate that this node has been selected for viewing. The contents of the node appear in the right hand part of the screen, a separate scrolling window.

with an average of one access per member. People and tasks, however, being more concerned with the immediate future and being more personal, tend to be accessed and updated more frequently. Even here, though, the *access rate* was less than one per day and updating was infrequent.

It was evident from the field study that individuals required the clearest possible organizational structure with clear roles, a plan structure that is simple to understand and relate to, and an efficient communication mechanism to coordinate members' work. The Plan Document was refined to make optimal use of the facilities of MUCH. A more significant change was made in the presentation of planning and timetabling of objectives. The translation of long-term visions into short-term objectives and *weekly schedules* was introduced. Because however, the longer term visions and objectives (down to 4 months) should require only infrequent consultation

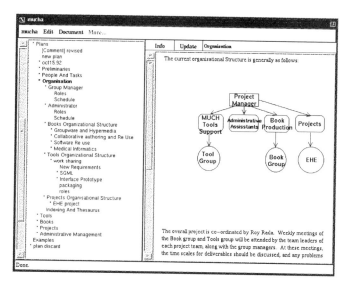

Figure 6.11: *Organization Nodes.* This outline shows the internal structure of the nodes in the Organization section, by way of example.

and amendment, as indicated by the statistical measures, it was decided that they should be in a separate document from the weekly schedules. The organizational principle chosen for the longer-term plans was the group activity base, composed of external relations, research, publications, tools, teaching, and internal relations (see Figure 6.12).

In the short-term (weekly) documents, members share in the establishment of weekly aims, and take responsibility for monitoring their own progress. According to this plan, the role of group managers is to assist in the establishment of weekly plans, reviewing and evaluating progress and adapting the schedules as required in the light of actual developments (see Figure 6.13). *Group managers* report on their group's progress at weekly, face-to-face management meetings. They are also involved in ensuring that current activities are in accordance with (mapped against) the visions and objectives and that these are being performed. The weekly meetings are also a useful forum for the presentation of suggestions and new ideas that may in turn influence the longer term visions and objectives.

To continue its growth, the MUCH organization has realized the need to take a number of steps, and these are:

- Acknowledgment of the need to manage the interaction between people and technical systems;
- Maintenance of a historical perspective, learning from the past and implementing changes accordingly;
- Decentralizing management;
- Encouraging people to manage themselves in small groups and take responsibility for their own development and motivation; and
- Being sensitive to the fact that there are no global solutions but that the solution has to be developed to fit the organization and must adapt as things change.

The efforts of the MUCH organization have demonstrated that it is possible to build a learning organization which focuses on courseware development in the context of a University Research Department. The cycle of evaluation followed by change and the adoption of *technological support* has led to new productivity.

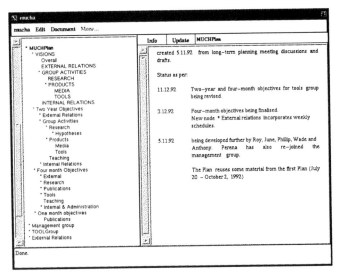

Figure 6.12: *Second Plan Document* This screen illustrates the structure and outline of the new Plan Document. The structures of visions, 2-year objectives and 4-month objectives are consistent and near identical.

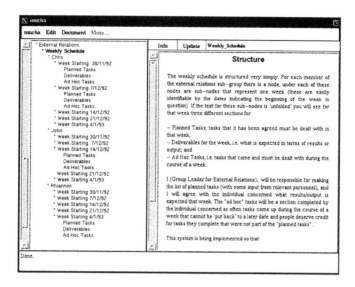

Figure 6.13: *External Relations Group.* This screen shows the External Relations Document, specifically designed for the External Relations Group. At any point it is possible for any group member to inspect the nodes and see what the group and its individual members are working on in the short term, for the current week as well as in previous weeks.

6.3 Exploiting the WWW

Usage of the World Wide Web (WWW) has grown exponentially in the early 1990s. The WWW can be used in coordinating the authoring educational hypermedia and in reusing existing hypermedia. The next sections will report on three developments within the WWW.

6.3.1 Assignment

A *classroom* assignment gave students the opportunity to work together as small organizations or companies. Each student was a member of a small company, and within that company the student was assigned to a group.

Each company had at least these groups:

• management

- information finding
- collaborative authoring

The company goal was to coherently link WWW information. Information was found, collected, and adapted to a new product. Additionally, the organization needed to communicate effectively, assign tasks properly, and monitor progress so that the assignment was completed to schedule and specification.

From a class of 60 students, 4 companies of 15 people each were formed by randomly assigning students to organizations. Two organizations developed products about medical therapies. The other two organizations converted two course textbooks from the MUCH system format into WWW format and then augmented the textbooks with relevant material from the WWW. The home page of each organization was stored in a directory of one of the team members. The resulting *WWW products* were also destined for delivery on a CD-ROM and thus should have been about 600 megabytes in size.

6.3.2   Individual Report and Peer-Peer Assessment

Each student's final mark was broken into three, equal parts: individual report, peer-peer assessment, and company product. For the individual report, each student discussed his group's ehavior and his role in the group and related this description to information in the course book about how group's behave. The student also described how and why his group did or did not use information technology to support its work and related this to the descriptions in the book. The student also discussed his organization's behavior and his group's activities within the organization. Individual reports were submitted by e-mail or stored as WWW pages (see Figure 6.14).

Each company submitted a grade for each of its members. The assessment was accompanied with written explanation as to why the grade was given to each person. How these grades were produced within the company was left to the discretion of the company. In one approach a group leader assigned someone within the group to the assessor role and reviewed the work of the assessor. A student's *peer assessment* typically included comments from the student's manager and other members of the student's group (see Figure "Peer-peer Assessment").

6.3.3   Final Product

The assessment of each company's final *WWW product* was equally divided among the following four criteria:

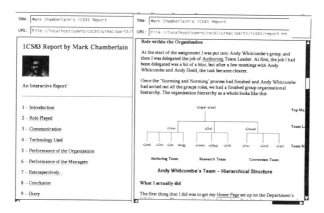

Figure 6.14: *WWW Individual Report:* These two windows from the WWW show on the left the cover page of the individual report of Mark Chamberlain. On the right is the node that stems from the link 'Role Played' on the left.

- completeness of the documentation. The home page must provide ready access to documentation explaining:
  - how this product was made,
  - how the user is expected to access the information, and
  - details about exactly how many megabytes of material can be reached from the home page and all the links to which it connects;

- gracefulness of WWW features in the product (understandable links leading to screens of meaningful information with adequate graphics, branching factors, and so on);
- closeness to the 600 megabyte target; and
- logical meaningfulness of the superstructure of the product as manifested either by:
  - conversion of the books (for the two companies that dealt with the course books) or
  - meaningful superstructure for health-care information (for the two companies that made health-care information products).

The final product was delivered by sending e-mail to the instructor with instructions of how to invoke the product home page.

Mark Beaumont is Group Leader of the Conversion Group. His peer-peer assessment
was ABOVE AVERAGE with the following justifi-
cation:

*   Management comment: ABOVE AVERAGE.
    Good leader. Worked Hard. Took an ef-
    ficient and professional approach.
    Managed to solve the majority of prob-
    lems within the group. Unambiguous
    with tasks that he delegated to the
    members in his group.
*   Comment from group member Adam Ryan:
    AVERAGE. Justification: Mark was
    helpful whenever it was needed. He did
    all the necessary work. He made sure
    everyone new what they were meant to
    do. He allowed you to work at your own
    pace as long as deadlines were reached.
*   Comment from group member M.R. Hempen-
    stall: ABOVE AVERAGE. Justifica-
    tion: Mark was very clear when it came
    to giving instructions and sent en-
    couraging messages and reminders when
    work was due. He shared the work out
    fairly and made sure we were happy with
    what we were doing and stayed in regu-
    lar contact.

Figure 6.15: *Peer-Peer Assessment*: This text was directly extracted
from the peer-peer assessment document submitted by one of the
companies to the teacher. The student Mark Beaumont received an
above average mark as a compilation of the marks from his manager
and the people who worked in his group (of which comments from
only two are shown here).

Copies of *screen images* from the final products are provided to indicate the character
of the work. The home page had a link to the documentation of the product and the
main contents of the product (see Figure 6.16). The WWW information also included
project work flow information (see Figure 6.17). The outlines for the medical
products were written by the students and contained pointers to information elsewhere
on the WWW (see Figure 6.18).

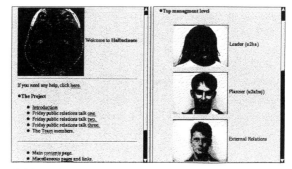

Figure 6.16: *Hallucinate Home Page:* One team called itself and its product 'Hallucinate'. The home page on the left included a pointer to 'Team'. Part of the node which was retrieved on selecting 'Team' is shown on the right-hand side of this screen as photos of three members of the top-management group and their roles.

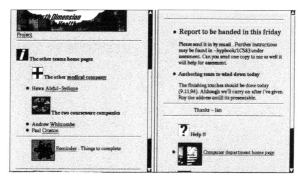

Figure 6.17: *Things to Complete:* These two windows from the WWW information of the student company which called itself 'The Fourth Dimension of Health-Care Technology' show on the left an icon for 'Reminder: Things to Complete' and on the right the result of selecting this icon. The window on the right shows requests from the leader of the company for reports from team members.

The student companies that made products based on the electronic books of the course followed a similar strategy to the medical companies for their home page. Namely, the home page contained pointers to documentation about the product and to the book content. Unlike the medical companies, the *book companies* needed to convert the books from their native MUCH format into WWW format (see Figure 6.20). The company was responsible to find information from the WWW related to the book and to make pointers from the book to that other WWW information (see Figure 6.19).

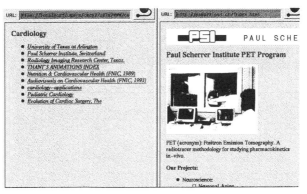

Figure 6.18: *Pointer to elsewhere on WWW*: The window on the right is a subsection of the table of contents of the 'The Fourth Dimension of Health Care Technology' product. This table of contents was stored in a student file at 'file://localhost/users/csc92/u2ls/WWW/cardiology'. On selecting the heading 'Paul Scherrer Institute of Switzerland', the user would be taken to the node at 'http://pss023.psi.ch/index.html' and get an introduction to the 'Paul Scherrer Institute PET Program'.

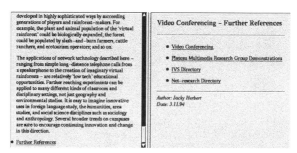

Figure 6.19: *Pointers from Book to WWW*: These two windows from the 'Courseware Development' product show on the left the bottom of a sub-section within the 'Coordination' chapter and on the right the result of clicking on the link 'Further References' which is at the bottom of the left window. Such 'Further References' were put at the end of each subsection of the book and led to related information on the WWW.

6.4   Refined WWW Projects

The WWW, particularly with tools such as Mosaic and with the proper social protocols, can be used as a coordination and reuse vehicle for electronic publishing. To further demonstrate this claim, another set of electronic products are being produced and a suite of tools are being developed that depend on the WWW.

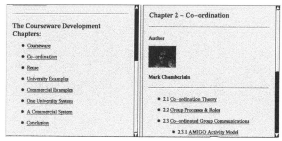

Figure 6.20: *Converted Book*: This screen comes from the company that used the 'Courseware Development' book. That book was an early draft of this book. The window on the left shows the table of the contents of the book in the WWW and the window on the right appears after the selection of the second chapter 'Coordination'.

6.4.1   Logical Structure

One problem with the WWW is that the logical structure of information is not addressed. The *Hypertext Markup Language* (HTML) with which WWW material is marked gives limited facility for logical structuring and focuses on the defining of arbitrary links from location to location. However the Standard General Markup Language (SGML) on which HTML is based is designed for specification of logical structure. In fact, as mentioned earlier in this book, HTML is a Document Type Definition (DTD) of SGML.

The *HTML DTD* can be extended to specify the logical structure of a hypermedia document. The resultant DTD is no longer equivalent to that for HTML but can incorporate HTML features for presentation purposes and for conformity with the WWW more generally. Once a document has been authored which is intended to conform to this DTD, a public domain SGML parser can be run on the document to test that the document indeed conforms to the DTD. Then the document can be automatically or semiautomatically converted into HTML form for delivery as a WWW product.

6.4.2   Manuals and Courseware

The logical structure of manuals has been carefully defined by various groups working with the American military. The logistics support sector of the military is a major purchaser of equipment and documentation for that equipment. To encourage uniformity that would in turn lead to reduced maintenance costs, increased reusability, and so on, the military has required that providers of documents provide them in electronic form and compliant to a military *maintenance manual* SGML DTD.

Companies that make maintenance manuals may often also want to produce training material to accompany the maintenance manuals. How can these companies take advantage of the maintenance manual and reuse it in making the *training material* or courseware? The difficulty in answering the question stems in part from the difficulty in defining a structure for courseware. In one case a piece of courseware differs from a manual in that it includes questions and answers which allow the student to test what has been learned. In another case, the courseware is based on a complex model of the real world and the user can interact with a simulation of this model in a way that supports trail-and-error learning.

For the case of a manual simply augmented with questions and answers, the DTD for courseware is readily derived from the DTD for the manual on which the course is based. For the opposite case, where the course is very sophisticated, the course may be seen as an algorithm or flowchart. The links in the *flowchart* might also point to portions of the manual to provide the user of the courseware with additional information.

Two *electronic products* are being developed consistent with the method thus far described. One is based on the Merck Medical Manual [119] and the other on a set of WWW manuals, such as the WN Server Manual [38]. In each case a DTD for the manuals is produced.

The products that are being developed will be essentially tailored material from the WWW. A *CD-ROM* will be made for both the medical information and for the information about the WWW itself. The publishers of the information will also mount the products on WWW servers. Furthermore, a paper book of about 160 pages will be prepared to accompany the CD-ROM and serve as a kind of extended table of contents.

6.4.3   Working Information Space

Two kinds of information need to be managed in the *information space* of the project: work-flow-related information and product information. Work-flow information includes the plan of work, the guidelines of quality, and the communications among staff. The product information includes the outline of the product and the drafts of the product. To be consistent with the exploitation of the WWW, all this information is stored on the WWW.

Members of the team are given a special *computer account.* Files on this account are stored with write and read permission for all members of the group, but are inaccessible to anyone who is not a member of group. Members of the team who want private information can store that on their personal accounts.

The work-flow information includes a discussion document in Issue-Based Information System format [119]. Quality standards include that all material is understandable, that a consistent format is followed, and that testing is regularly done. To facilitate the collaborative work on the product, the *product information* is extensively decomposed so that only small chunks of material are being edited at one time by one person. If an author is editing a file, then others are not able to edit it till the author surrenders control.

6.4.4   Roles

Execution of the work plan includes the assignment of people to *roles*. Managers of the project must monitor this assignment of people to roles so that assignments can change as some work goes faster or slower than expected. The six roles that are here identified include author, librarian, copyright specialist, marketing specialist, acquisition specialist, and formatter. Further descriptions of the roles follow:

Author: The authors determine the logical structure of the product, prepare the spine of the material, and collaborate with others in integrating information from the WWW into the product. Numerous tools exist for authoring in SGML and HTML, and the authors are free to use whatever tools they want. The structure of the resultant HTML documents is not arbitrary however, and authors must follow a fixed style. The style is defined initially in an SGML way and authors can use a SGML DTD to guide their work.

Librarian: The librarian role within the team is for finding relevant information on the WWW. The librarian must work closely with the authors. The librarian must also clearly identify the size in megabytes of whatever is identified.

Copyright specialist: Material that is identified as relevant to the new product will only be included in the product, if the owners agree that it can be included on the CD-ROM. The owners will not surrender ownership but the publisher of the CD will require permission of the owner to reproduce the information on the CD. In other words, the publisher must have the right to copy the material, while the owner also retains the right to copy it. The role of the copyright specialist is to establish communication with the owners of information and to seek their formal approval of the copyright agreement.

Marketing specialist: The marketing specialist must maintain contact with the publisher and potential users. The arrangements with contributors to the product for the sharing of any royalties is also managed by the marketing specialist.

Acquisition specialist: Information that is to be reused will be acquired by the acquisition specialist.   After the information is copied to the local site where the authoring continues, the links are renamed to fit with the local site and the CD-ROM.

Formatter: A separate media index is maintained.   The CD includes public domain viewers which can be used with the media that are provided with the CD.   Various converters exist for images and sound and they will be exploited.   The role of the formatter is to maintain the media index, to acquire and locally install public domain viewers, and to convert media, as necessary, from one format to another.

Other typical roles are also required, such as leader of the team.   The people who compose the team will play these various roles.

6.4.5   SIGBIO CD-ROM

A procedure similar to that outlined for the work of students in making WWW products was followed by a group of staff at the University of Liverpool to collect material from the WWW and to make a CD-ROM [113] of that material.   The title of the CD is   *Medical Multimedia and Informatics* (see Figure 6.21) and   it was published in December, 1994 along with a newsletter [114] that explained the product. The work was done as a volunteer effort for the Association of Computing Machinery (ACM) Special Interest Group in Biomedical Computing (SIGBIO).

The work occurred in the following ways:

*   Information from the WWW was identified as relevant to the topic.
*   Owners of this relevant information were contacted and formally asked for permission to include their material in the new CD.
*   Information was copied via ftp from the site that it normally inhabited to the site where the CD was being made.
*   The link names in the copied information were changed so that they would no longer point to the original host but now to the local CD.
*   Installation and user guide documentation was produced for the CD.
*   A CD was premastered and tested.
*   The premaster went to mass production, and 1,000 CDs were then mailed to SIGBIO members and libraries.

The CD has elicited numerous comments for those who have seen it.   Unfortunately, the *installation guides* were not clear and when contrasted to a successful commercial product the SIGBIO CD is not easy to start using.   Once people have mastered the installation, they seem impressed with the content of the CD and with the idea of thus bundling WWW information.

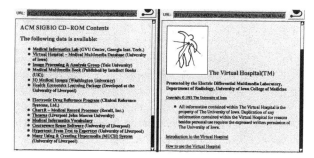

Figure 6.21: *SIGBIO CD:* The window on the left is a view of the Table of Contents of the SIGBIO CD-ROM — in this case the information is stored on the local site '/cs/formby2/rrpc/Sigbio-ok'. When the user clicks on the node 'Virtual Hospital — Medical Multimedia Database (University of Iowa)' the information in the right window appears. The material on the right was copied (with permission) from the University of Iowa and installed at /cs/formby2/rrpc/Sigbio-ok and also placed on the SIGBIO CD-ROM.

6.5   Conclusion

The Many Using and Creating Hypermedia (MUCH) system represents a sophisticated *application* of hypermedia and groupware to the coordination of people and the reuse of educational material in a university setting. Other systems elsewhere would have strengths that the MUCH system does not have. Nevertheless, the MUCH system illustrates several interesting features of a technological tool for courseware development. More importantly, the MUCH system has been extensively used and this chapter has documented several applications of the MUCH system.

The *MUCH system* has undergone multiple revisions since the mid-1980s. Since the early 1990s, the system architecture has been based on the popular hypermedia model (the Dexter model of Chapter 1) that separates the interface from the logical model of the hypermedia, which in turn is separated from the raw content. Extensive experience with authors and students has lead to the refinement of an interface which emphasizes simplicity and hierarchical views. Additionally, the value of paper versions of material wherever practical to go hand-in-hand with computer versions has been found desirable and is explicitly and well-supported by the MUCH system functions for importing and exporting material.

The MUCH system was used in writing this book and several other textbooks. In this way, the system served in large part as a common database of the evolving hypertexts. Numerous staff and students have been able to browse and comment on the content. Classes have studied the material online and done their exercises on the MUCH system. In this way, the system has been simultaneously an *authoring environment* and a delivery environment.

As the MUCH group grew in size, it needed to develop additional ways of managing itself. The MUCH group has actually become an 'organization', namely a set of tightly connected groups that address a common vision. This new entity, the *MUCH organization,* faced management problems and its experience sheds light on some of the potential problems that may be encountered by university courseware groups as they expand and attempt to employ computer support to facilitate this expansion.

The weaknesses of the MUCH system include that it is a university prototype which is not widely supported. Users must learn about the MUCH system especially for the purposes of working with the MUCH staff. Other tools that may have fewer features than the MUCH system, such as the World Wide Web, are much more widely used and have thus compelling advantages. Furthermore, one of the major lessons of the MUCH experiences is that the methods by which people work together are more important than the tools that they use. People who work well together and have a clear plan will get far more done than people who are not well coordinated but have sophisticated tools. Accordingly, the role of the WWW as a coordination and reuse tool is being extensively investigated.

This chapter has reported on three projects that depended on coordination of a team of people and reuse of hypermedia through and from the WWW. One occurred with a class of 60 students who worked as teams in making new WWW products. In another development, students worked together to convert manuals into WWW educational hypermedia. In a final development a CD-ROM of WWW material was produced for the Association of Computing Machinery Special Interest Group in Biomedical Computing. The students and staff who use the WWW are immediately impressed with the wide range of information available on the WWW and the rapid growth of new features on the WWW. Many tools are being developed by universities and contributed freely to the Internet community for use with the WWW. The WWW readily supports the *coordinated authoring* and *reuse* of educational hypermedia.

7
Commercial Systems

The commercial examples (see Chapter 5) have guided the design and implementation of computer systems to support commercial courseware development. One such system focused on reuse and was developed with a simple hypermedia tool. The other system, called the Open System for Collaborative Authoring and Reuse is one of the most advanced systems of its type in the world today.

7.1   A Courseware Reuse System

A number of companies and educational institutions develop courseware. One such company is Integrated Radiological Services Limited (IRS Ltd.), a small company with 17 employees. IRS Ltd. specializes in diagnostic radiology but has two employees who author courseware. Courseware authors at IRS Ltd. appreciate the value of courseware reuse as a potential solution to decreasing the time and money spent on courseware development.

IRS Ltd. has a large number of *reusable components* around the office such as books, papers, word processed files, magazines, diagrams in electronic format, spreadsheets, photographs of equipment that they have developed themselves, graphs, tables, references, questions/answers, and computer programs. The majority of this material is not currently being used by courseware developers at IRS Ltd., even though the material is potentially useful and relevant.

IRS Ltd. wanted to find ways in which courseware authoring could be improved through the process of reuse. Accordingly IRS Ltd. contracted the development of a *reuse* system that stores reusable components, provides authors with efficient and rapid retrieval mechanisms, possesses an interface which makes the addition of components to the database straightforward, and incorporates other reuse features. In this way, IRS Ltd. believed resources such as time and money used in the authoring process for courseware would be substantially reduced.

7.1.1   Media to be Reused

Authors at IRS Ltd. have identified eight types of material that they want the reusable courseware library to contain: text, diagrams, photographs, graphs, tables, references, questions/answers, and programs. The material which is to be reused is not always in a format that is immediately compatible with the courseware library into which it is to be included. Material to be reused must be *converted* into a format that is compatible with the required courseware library, before it can be entered.

Text, programs, and references present themselves in a wide variety of formats. Text that is to be reused from books and magazines must first be scanned, using an electronic scanner, and converted to an appropriate format. ToolBook possesses an *import* facility that allows text which is in ASCII format to be automatically imported into the authoring package. Text in word processed files must first be converted to an ASCII format and then entered into ToolBook.

Diagrams can be found in books, magazines, or in an electronic format. Diagrams that are paper-based are first scanned. The scanned image is saved in an appropriate format, and then converted to a format that is compatible with ToolBook. ToolBook possesses an *importgraphic* function that allows diagrams in various formats to be imported. For the purposes of this courseware library, all diagrams must be converted to a bitmap format before they can be included within the library. This can be done with a package such as Graphic Workshop, which allows diagrams to be converted from one format to another and also facilitates the cropping, scaling,a and so on of the diagrams (see Figure 7.1).

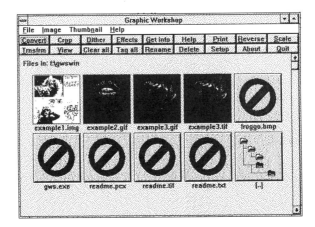

Figure 7.1: *Screen Images.* Screen image showing the facilities provided by Graphics Workshop.

Graphs and tables are also converted to bitmap format before being entered into the courseware library. As graphs and tables usually possess numbers that can sometimes be very small, they must be scaled upwards, so that they can be legibly read. However, there is a limit to the size of reusable courseware components, as they should not exceed the size of the screen. It is sometimes the case that certain graphs and tables cannot be reused simply because the scanner used is not of a good enough quality to produce images that are *legible* and if the images are scaled upwards so that they become legible, then they are too big to fit on the screen.

The conversion of questions and answers to a format where they can be used within the courseware library is similar to that of text in that the questions and answers must first be converted to a plain text format before they can be reused. However, it is often the case that when *questions and answers* appear in books, there is often a page of questions and a separate page of answers. Thus, if the author wishes to access a question and its answer, the questions and answers will have to be linked.

7.1.2 Retrieval

The reusable courseware library possesses two types of organization, which are designed to complement each other:

* Media Index
* Table of Contents

The *media index* allows the author to select the type of media he wishes the retrieved component to be. Furthermore, each component has text associated with it, which can be up to 25 words long.

After the author enters the type of medium to retrieve, the author enters keywords(s), describing the topic on which to retrieve components. A search is then conducted of all the components of that media type within the library. If the author selects *photograph* from the media index and then enters a keyword such as *burn*, a search is made of all of the photographs within the library. A list of all text fields associated with the photographs that possess the keyword *burn* is displayed. The author can select the required text field from the list and the associated photograph is displayed for the author. If the author wishes to view the other photographs in the list of components retrieved by the system, he can click on *next* and *previous* buttons (see Figure 7.2), which are features of each screen possessing a reusable component and move through the list. Retrieval of components of other media, using the media index, is done in a similar fashion. Figure 7.3 shows how the logical model of the media index is designed.

The *table of contents* is generated through the reuse of the table of contents of a book, on the topic of the courseware library. This reusable courseware library possesses a table of contents that incorporates the main topics within the field of diagnostic radiology. When components on a particular subject are entered into the library, a more specific table of contents can be generated by incorporating the table of contents of a book on the subject into the more general table of contents of the library.

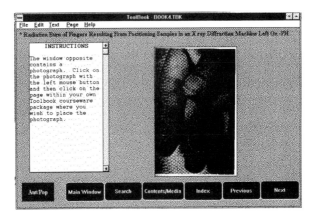

Figure 7.2: *Typical Screen of the Reusable Courseware Library.* Image showing the facilities available for the author's use on a typical screen of the reusable courseware library.

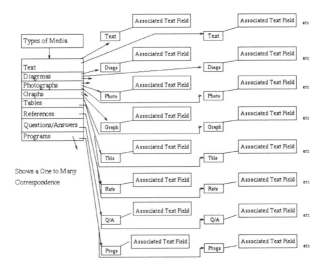

Figure 7.3: *Logical Model of the Media Index.* Each media type points to multiple media components, and each component has an associated text field.

Authors are able to retrieve relevant material from the library be selecting a *heading* from the table of contents. A list is displayed of all of the components within the library that satisfy the author's request. Figure 7.4 shows how the logical model of the table of contents is designed. Each heading in the table of contents corresponds to many reusable components of different media types.

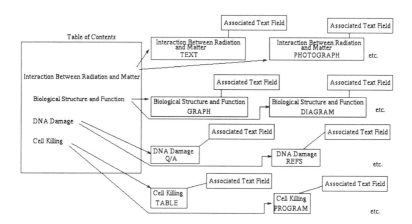

Figure 7.4: *Logical Model of the Table of Contents.* The entries in the Table of Contents on the left point to reusable components on the right.

7.1.3 Interface

IRS Ltd. develop their courseware using the authoring package *ToolBook*. The reuse system was also built with ToolBook. The retrieval tool itself uses one instance of a ToolBook window, and the courseware to be developed by the author uses another instance of a ToolBook window (see Figure 7.5). Material to be reused is transferred from the reusable courseware library to the courseware being developed by the author.

The transfer of text from one ToolBook instance to another is made possible by ToolBook's own cutting and pasting facilities. Authors select the text to be transferred, select the *copy* option from a menubar within ToolBook, then move to their own courseware, and select *paste* from a menubar on the page on which they wish the text to appear. The text is then transferred to the author's courseware.

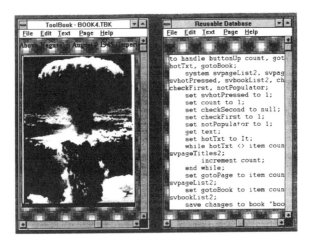

Figure 7.5: *Two Instances of a ToolBook Window.* Screen image showing two instances of a ToolBook window.

Diagrams, photographs, graphs, and tables are all stored as bitmap files within ToolBook. To transfer these *images* to his own courseware, an author clicks on the component he wishes to transfer and then clicks on the page within his courseware where he wishes the new component to appear. The image is then transferred to the courseware.

Programs in the reuse library may be in various programming languages. The transfer of these *programs* to the author's courseware is the same as that for text. The courseware library also possesses programs written in ToolBook's own programming language, OpenScript, which authors may automatically place behind buttons.

The *scenario* for the use of the courseware library by the author of the tool is:

- Author selects the type of access to the library i.e., table of contents or media index (see Figure 7.6).
- If he wishes to use the table of contents, then he selects a heading from the table of contents within the library and then a list of candidate components is revealed through which he can browse. Alternatively, if he wishes to use the media index, he is asked to enter a keyword, at which point a list of candidate components is displayed through which the author can browse.

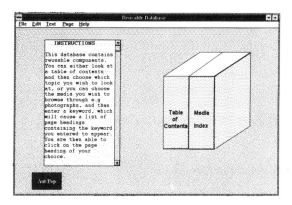

Figure 7.6: *Retrieval Mechanisms.* Shows the Retrieval Mechanisms provided for the author.

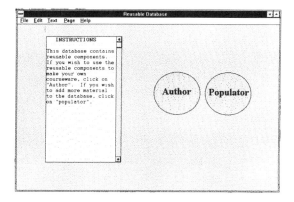

Figure 7.7: *First Window.* Screen image showing the first window in the library.

Figure 7.8: *Table of Contents Page.* Screen image showing the Table of Contents page.

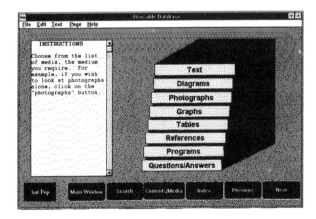

Figure 7.9: *Media Index Page.* Screen image showing the Media Index page.

When authoring is finished, the author can click a button to take him to the first page in the library (see Figure 7.7). Additionally, authors can also return to the list of possible candidate components generated by the retrieval mechanisms, to the table of contents page (see Figure 7.8), or the media index page (see Figure 7.9).

There are two sides to the reusable courseware library the authoring side, and the populator side. The authoring side is concerned with the retrieval of reusable components from the library. The populator is presented with the window shown in Figure 7.7 and after choosing the *Populator* button, is then given a choice of media with which to populate the library. He is then required to enter the filename of the file possessing the required component. The component is then automatically entered into the library. The populator is also required to place a text caption with the component.

The IRS Ltd. reuse system was extensively tested. A small library was created, and courseware was authored via reuse of the library components. Authors found both the media index and the table of contents to be important — neither alone was enough. However, given the diverse training requirements and the cost of populating the library, authors are not clear as to whether the reuse system will or will not prove cost effective to IRS Ltd. in the long run.

7.2   OSCAR Architecture

The *Open System for Collaborative Authoring and Reuse* (OSCAR) project was based on observations of businesses that develop courseware. The OSCAR project was funded by the European Union and several companies throughout Europe. The product of the OSCAR project was a system to support coordinated authoring and resue of courseware.

In the OSCAR system the following processing environments are defined:

* the authoring workstation
* the workgroup environment
* the courseware project environment

The *authoring workstation* is the execution environment of an authoring application and represents the physical workplace of an individual author. The authoring workstation is essentially based on a multimedia personal computer.

The *workgroup environment* supports a group working on strictly related activities, using common information, and sharing physical devices, applications, and communication facilities. Within a workgroup environment, local authoring workstations are networked by means of a Local Area Net. Remote authoring workstations can also be connected to the workgroup environment via the Integrated Services Digital Network. The *courseware project environment* supports several workgroups cooperating in a given project over several sites, even remotely located. The workgroups perform parallel development of pieces of courseware or execute different activities of the courseware development process. In both cases they need to exchange information and integrate their results (see Figure 7.10).

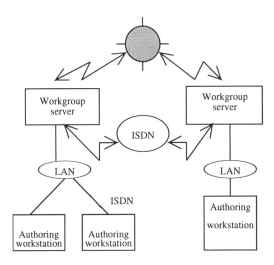

Figure 7.10: *The OSCAR Courseware Project Environment.* The Courseware Project Environment supports workgroups. LAN means Local Area Network. ISDN means Integrated Services Digital Network. The darkened circle at the top represents a satellite that is an alternate communication link between two workgroup services.

The *OSCAR architecture* represents the way in which the OSCAR services are organized, what functional level they realize, and what relationship exists between them. To better represent the organization of services provided by OSCAR, and the relationship between them, OSCAR services have been grouped in layers. Layers are stacked one on the other following an increasing level of abstraction of the services offered (see Figure 7.11). Within a layer a *space* offers a collection of services that contribute to the same general objective, and a component represents a well-defined set of functionalities that can be used as a single block.

OSCAR provides the following layers:

- *Hardware Platform:* contains all hardware components supported by OSCAR;
- *Operating System:* contains the operating systems supported by OSCAR on the various hardware platforms;
- *Communication Space:* provides services supporting the distribution of the system and the network management;
- *Common Information Space:* supplies information management services relevant to the courseware development process;
- *Coauthoring Space:* this layer provides high-level services to support authoring of multimedia courseware, coordination, collaboration, codecision and reuse in courseware development; and
- *Author Desktop:* provides the presentation functions that allow an application to interact with people in a consistent and intuitive way.

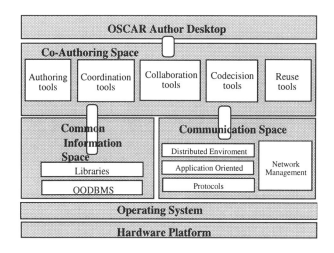

Figure 7.11: *The OSCAR Layers.* Five layers are depicted here. The user directly sees the author desktop. OODBMS means object-oriented database management system.

In OSCAR a *client/server* approach has been adopted. In the client/server representation, applications are typically split in two parts: the front end, which runs on the client workstation and implements the direct interface to the user, and the back end, which is the part that runs on the server and implements the core functionalities of the application (see Figure 7.12). Although most services have code residing both on the workstation and on the server, the services considered as the infrastructure of the client/server model are mainly executed on the server. They include the object-oriented database management system and the communication functions. The co-authoring services are mainly present on the client workstation.

The flexibility of the OSCAR client/server platform means that:

- servers can support many client workstations
- workstations can simultaneously access multiple databases on many servers
- server and client can be coresident on the same machine

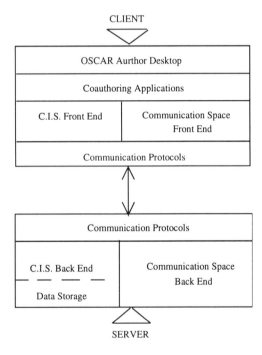

Figure 7.12: *Client/Server View.* Applications are split in two parts: the front end which runs on the client workstation and implements the direct interface to the user, and the back end, which runs on the server and implements the core functionalities of the application. CIS means Common Information Space.

Client workstations represent the user entry point into the OSCAR system. The OSCAR *client workstations* are mainly multimedia personal computers on which coauthoring applications run. They can be remotely connected to allow a distant author to get access to the OSCAR services. The OSCAR *server* provides multiuser services in the distributed environment. Unix serves as the multitasking, multiuser operating system. MS-Windows is the reference operating system for the client workstation.

The *OSCAR Author Desktop* (OAD) provides the interface for the author. The mouse and the keyboard are the devices available for the user's input, whereas the computer monitor and the loudspeakers are used for output. Each OSCAR user interface is autocustomizable and displays only the tools, the commands, and the options required by the user profile. After installation an OSCAR icon is presented, and double clicking on this icon executes the OSCAR application. A message box requiring the users login data (username password, project) is then automatically displayed (see Figure 7.13). If the username and the password are correct, the login message box will disappear and the customized OAD will be displayed.

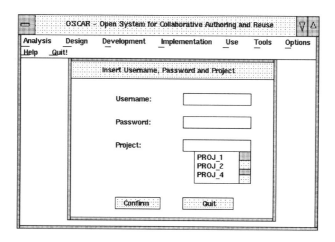

Figure 7.13: *Message Box.* The user initially specifies his username, password, and the project on which he works.

7.3   Information and Communication Spaces

The OSCAR *Common Information Space* (CIS) allows different software components and different users of the system to share information, update the information consistently, and base their work on the work of other actors. Reusability is based on the ability of the CIS to store material that can be retrieved and reused in contexts and with purposes different from the original ones.

The CIS includes an 'instructional component' and a 'presentational component', whose trait d' union is the Instructional Object. Schematically, the Instructional Component includes:

- Domain Objects
- Student Modeling Objects

On the other hand, the Presentational Component specifies the physical representation of the actual learning material.

A *multimedia unit* (MMU) is a composition in space and time of several *monomedia units* (MUs). Examples of MMUs are pictures with captions, but also couples or triples of pictures, and pictures with voice. A single picture, a text, or a sound sequence are examples of MUs (see Figure 7.14). Of course, there is a need for an object that specifies how several MUs can be combined in space and time to make a MMU. Such an object should also be able to handle small interactions among MUs and diversified exits from a MMU. This object is called 'layout', and it has been defined as a separate object to allow an author to present the same MMU in different ways, and various MMUs in the same way (see Figure 7.15).

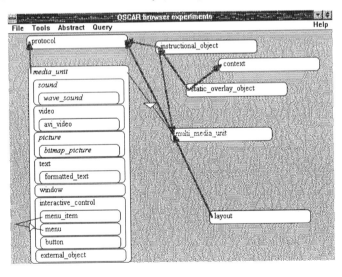

Figure 7.14: *Screen onto Media Units.* This screen dump from the OSCAR system shows some of the features of the CIS, particularly media units.

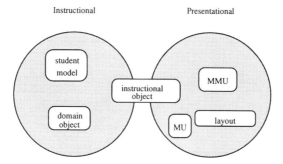

Figure 7.15: *Two Components of the CIS.* MMU is multimedia unit. MU is monomedia unit. Layout determines how a media unit appears on the screen.

The CIS includes a pedagogical classification schema for browsing the multimedia database of learning material [99]. This *pedagogical classification schema* functions as a kind of domain-specific filter between users and the CIS. A unit of learning material (ULM) represents a collection of MMUs. A ULM is characterized by the pedagogical classification schema in terms of pedagogical attributes such as source, identification, quality level, and completeness (see Figure 7.16). The production of courseware consists of designing a courseware structure and selecting or producing suitable ULMs.

A flexible and powerful description and classification schema is necessary for the purpose of efficient retrieval and reuse of ULMs. Semantic description of a ULM is an important aspect of the schema. For instance, the user should be able to formulate queries in terms of meanings of targeted ULMs, such as 'an image with a rainbow' and 'a video clip about the Challenger space shuttle'. In order to provide efficient and effective support for retrieval and reuse of multimedia objects, the system should be sufficiently flexible so that the chosen level of attributes can be relaxed or tightened in response to the initial search result.

The *Reuse Services* support both the retrievability and the customization of training material. In particular, the functionalities offered by the Reuse Services include browsing functionalities, aimed at supporting accessibility and retrievability of the CIS objects, and conversion tools, to reuse material originally available in a format different from the desired one. With the conversion facility, the user who is examining a particular monomedia unit chooses some unit (see Figure 7.17). Then the user selects any of many available formats in which the unit should be stored. The system will then retrieve the monomedia unit from the database, automatically convert it into the desired format, and then store it as a file in the computer.

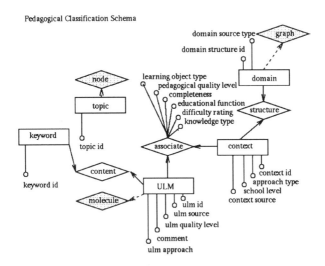

Figure 7.16: *ULM.* A pedagogical classification schema for retrieval and reuse of Units of Learning Material. Adapted from [99]. 'id' means identifier.

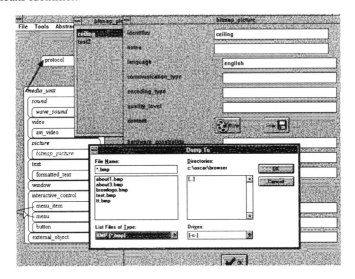

Figure 7.17: *Converter.* Screen dump from the OSCAR system which presents information about a particular image or bitmap and gives the user an option to convert that bitmap into a variety of formats.

The *Browser* allows a user to navigate and query the CIS, in accordance with well-defined indexing and classification methods. In principle, the Browser allows access to all the objects stored in the CIS, according to the user's access privileges. For this reason, it is necessary for the user to have some idea of the underlying CIS Conceptual Schema.

The OSCAR *Communication Space* must support the following functions:

* real-time transmission of multimedia data,
* exchange of information between actors involved in courseware projects, and
* real-time collaboration by actors working together in a given activity.

To support these functions, the communication space architecture has been organized in three layers:

1. The *Communication Layer* provides functionalities related to the aspects of physical connectivity. The multimedia communication is supported by this layer both over local and wide area networks (ISDN and satellite).
2. The *Application-Oriented Layer* contains the basic features needed to support the OSCAR Distributed Environment (client-server interaction mechanisms) as well as functionalities for supporting asynchronous and/or synchronous communication among OSCAR users. The security of the information over the network is also handled in this layer.
3. The *Distributed Environment Layer* makes use of the services of the underlying OSCAR Application-Oriented Layer, authenticates and authorizes users to access the system (Security and Authorization Service), and allows transparent access to remote files (Distributed File System).

An author who wants to access the full set of OSCAR services requires a high-bandwidth link.

7.4   Coordination Model

Based on the courseware authoring process described in Chapter 5, a *coordination model* may be represented in the Activity Model Environment (AME) modeling language that was described in Chapter 2 [134]. In AME intermediate products can be treated as messages. A message is created in a workspace with a template from the organizational manual. The message will contain information about who created it and the time it was created. The message is then routed again to an Instructional Designer workspace (see Figure 7.18). A partial description of the courseware life cycle is provided as an indication of how the AME model takes shape for OSCAR.

From the five basic phases of Analysis, Design, Development, Implementation, and Evaluation several subphases will be described in the AME model.

7.4.1   Learning Needs Analysis

The objective of the Learning Needs Analysis subphase of the 'Analysis' phase is to analyze the actual learning needs in order to define the general educational aims (knowledge, skills, and behaviors to be acquired by the learners) and the prerequisites to enter the course. In particular, the analysis of learning needs can be divided into the following tasks:

1.   to gather information about the target environment and the target population (using different modalities, such as interviews and questionnaires);
2.   to structure and aggregate the gathered information by statistical methods;
3.   to define the general educational aims and the content areas; and
4.   to define prerequisites to enter the course.

The *Customer/Sponsor Information message* is created by an Instructional Designer in his workspace using a template from the organizational manual. The message will contain information about the person who created it, the role the creator was playing (Instructional Designer), and the time it was created. The message is then routed again to an Instructional Designer workspace (see Figure 7.18). Typically, a person performs the role and fills in the details in the current unit of the message. However, some of the fields within the unit may be filled in automatically by the computer. After the person or the computer fills in the fields in the unit, the workspace unlocks the message and informs the current unit that it is complete. At this stage, the unit triggers its rules which check the validity of the field values and determine which will be the new 'current' unit and which role will process it. The message then routes itself to the appropriate workspace.

This circuit is repeated until all the units are completed. At this point the message is considered complete and the next message is activated and routed to the appropriate workspace. The process is repeated until the final Learner Needs Analysis is produced. Once the analysis of learning has been completed, the courseware outline may be developed.

7.4.2   Courseware Outline

The objective of the *Courseware Outline* subphase of the 'Analysis' phase is to define the overall courseware architecture as a framework for the design phase. At the same time it provides the information needed to estimate and plan the development effort (see Figure 7.19).

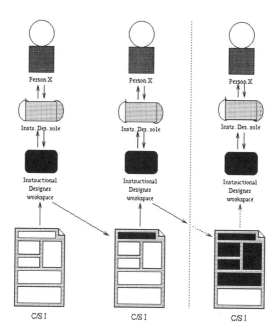

C/S I: Customer/Sponsor Information

Figure 7.18: *Context Analysis.* The Customer Information message contains information about its creator (Person X), their role (Instructional Designer), and the time it was created. This Figure shows how the message is routed to the Instructional Designer workspace.

The messages required to generate the courseware outline include those used in the 'Learner Needs Analysis' subphase and additionally Module Description Card 1, Module Description Card 2, and Architecture messages.

Three different roles collaborate to produce the courseware outline; namely, the Instructional Designer, the Subject Matter Expert, and the Media Expert in a two-stage process:

1. Messages completed in the 'learning needs analysis' subphase are manipulated to complete Module Development Cards 1 and 2.
2. Finally, the *Module Development Cards* lead to the completion of the Architecture.

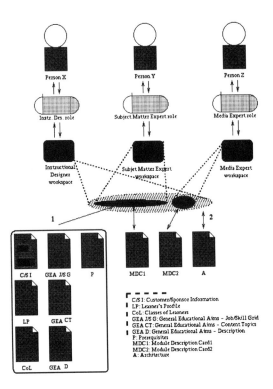

Figure 7.19: *Courseware Outline.* This AME model shows the messages shared by the Instructional Designer, Subject Matter Expert and Media Expert in the definition of courseware modules and the overall architecture.

The next and final phase of the analysis consists of planning the project using information obtained during the definition of the courseware outline.

7.4.3   Design

Following the Analysis phase, which clarifies requirements and produces the project plan, is the *Design* phase. This phase is concerned with specifying and defining the requirements so that they may be further developed. Several subphases of the Design phase, represented in the AME model, are next illustrated.

The aim of the *Contents Domain Representation* subphase is to represent the course content. The content's representation will match the educational objectives and will have a grain size that supports a modular architecture of the courseware. In addition, contents will have a high level of independence from both the instructional strategies and underlying technology (see Figure 7.20). The Subject Matter Expert and the Instructional Designer work together to process three messages: Specific Educational Objectives, Contents Domain Representation, and Architecture. The output from this activity is the completed Contents Domain Representation, taking into account the Educational Objectives.

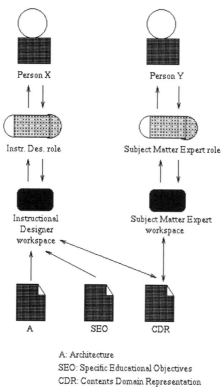

A: Architecture
SEO: Specific Educational Objectives
CDR: Contents Domain Representation

Figure 7.20: *Contents Domain Representation.* The Instructional Designer and the Subject Matter Expert collaborate to produce a Contents Domain Representation.

The aim of the *Instructional Strategies Definition* subphase is the analysis of the courseware matter in order to define and organize the presentation of the courseware contents to the learner, taking into account the possible didactic strategies related to its model. Once the Instructional Strategies have been defined, the Assessment Methods may be specified.

The objective of the *Definition of Assessment Methods* subphase is to define the interactions with the learner in order to:

* assess the learning
* define the current educational path on the basis of the learner's performance (see Figure 7.21).

The Subject Matter Expert, the Communication Expert, and the Instructional Designer work together to define the interactions and judge the answers. Messages in addition to 'Specific Educational Objectives' are 'Sequencing Networks', 'Documentation about Interactions', 'Strategies Networks', 'Feedback Documentation', and 'Relations between Educational Strategies and Learner Model'. This concludes the design stage and the outputs at this stage combine to form the pedagogical plan.

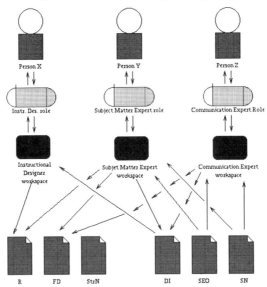

R: Relations between Educational Strategies and Learner Models
FD: Feedback Documentation
StrN: Strategies Networks
DI: Documentation about Interactions
SN: Sequencing Networks
SEO: Specific Educational Objectives

Figure 7.21: *Definition of Assessment Methods.* The Definition of Assessment Methods subphase involves messages on six different topics, as listed above.

7.4.4   Development

In the *Courseware Development* phase, guidelines for the implementation are established. The aim of the 'Standards' subphase is to define a set of guidelines that guarantee quality and uniformity of the development phase products. The objectives of the 'Script and Storyboard' subphase are to define and to describe the actual material involved in the courseware (textual, graphical, sound, and video) and to make available the global pattern of the screen layout and the flow of control through the program (see Figure 7.22).

The tasks of the *Script and Storyboarding* subphase are to produce the Script and the Storyboard. Messages involved are:

- Contents List,
- Architecture,
- Selected Educational Strategies,
- Contents Domain Representation,
- Specific Educational Objectives,
- Writing Standards,
- Script of Contents,
- General Standards,
- Storyboarding Draft Forms, and
- Storyboarding Production Forms.

Six roles are required in the 'Script and Storyboard' subphase: Graphics Designer, Media Expert, Subject Matter Expert, Communication Expert, Instructional Designer, and Writer. On completion of this phase, all the components of the technical plan have been assembled and implementation can proceed.

7.4.5   Implementation and Evaluation

In the *Implementation* phase, courseware will be implemented in accordance with the specifications defined in the storyboarding process (see Figure 7.23). This entails prototyping and implementing the multimedia courseware and checking its congruence with the specifications. The messages involved in this activity are:

- Courseware Detailed Description,
- Prototype, and
- Consistent Prototype.

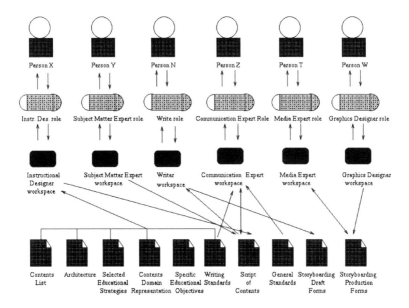

Figure 7.22: *Script.* This figure shows the interaction of roles and messages involved in producing the script.

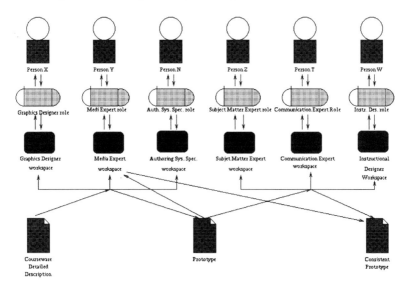

Figure 7.23: *Implementation.* This figure shows the wide range of roles involved in the implementation of the multimedia courseware, and how they work together to achieve this.

A wide range of roles are required to work together to perform the above tasks; namely, the Graphics Designer, the Media Expert, the Authoring System Specialist, the Subject Matter Expert, the Communication Expert, the Media Expert, and the Instructional Designer.

The implementation phase results in the final product, refined through prototyping, for testing, validation, and evaluation. In the Evaluation phase the Subject Matter Expert, the Instructional Designer, the Communication Expert, and the Media Expert conduct a quality review and pilot testing.

7.5   Coordination Services

The Coordination Services implement the coordination model. They are intended as services to manage the interdependencies between activities performed by multiple actors. In other words, they support the coordination of a project by setting up the whole environment, making work plans, and ensuring that people are able to cooperate at the right moment and with the needed information (see Figure 7.24).

The coordination services must provide to the users:

*   setup functionalities
*   runtime functionalities

The *setup functionalities* are related to the startup phase of the project, whereas the runtime functionalities support people while working on the project. The process of setting up and running a project, as far as the coordination services are concerned, begins when the project manager or someone that has an equivalent role creates a new project template and enters all the needed values for the attributes of the new Project Template. Then an authoring methodology and a set of quality standards must be chosen from the available ones or created from scratch.

After these two preliminary steps, the project can be 'officially' started by launching a module called the *Context Sensitive Module* (CSM). The CSM is able to read the *Project Template* in order to deduce from it the state of the project, that is to say which message objects have been produced and which message object(s) can be produced at the moment (i.e., the input they need is ready). The CSM puts in action the person(s) that must work to produce the message object(s) by looking into the Project Template and the electronic mail address(es) of the person(s) and sending:

- The Message Object Template,
- The Message Object(s) needed as input, and
- The list of persons collaborating on that task, if the task is performed by a team.

At this moment the work of the Coordination Services is suspended, the CSM 'goes to sleep' and waits until the *message object* is completed. The task of making people interact among themselves is up to the Collaboration and/or Codecision Services. When the message object is completed, someone 'wakes up' the CSM by passing to it the prepared message object (the completed template). Then the CSM marks in the Project Template the message object as produced, and starts again its cycle to deduce the new state of the project and so on.

A Project manager or anyone that has been allowed to do it can, at any moment during the project life cycle, ask of the CSM the *state of the project* to the present date or to a date somewhere in the future. The view that the CSM can give to the user can be on:

- the message objects (produced, to be produced, being produced);
- the Phases / Activities (finished, to be started, being carried on);
- the Roles / Persons (being engaged, that will be engaged).

The author can start his work from scratch by creating new objects, or he can start from an existing object. The system gives an author the possibility of working in a private space so that no one can disturb his work (no one can lock or modify the object under the control of that author). Furthermore the system gives an author a special view of an existing object, that is a version of an object.

The Coordination Service also supports an authoring team during technical discussions, providing it with proper mechanisms that should facilitate a group decision-making process. The problem is approached by defining both data structuring and retrieval mechanisms able to model the information flow during a team discussion (see Figure 7.25). Strictly speaking, this is a computer conferencing system specifically designed to support a group decision-making process in an authoring setting. As the Group Decision Support System deals with messages exchanged by actors, the CIS stores objects belonging to the message class, featuring attributes such as the subject and the contribution type such as evaluation, elaboration, information providing, or question answering. A *Discussion Path* is made of messages whose subjects are the same or related to one another. The actors who generate or receive messages may have different roles, such as initiator, contributor, or administrator, in the discussion path itself.

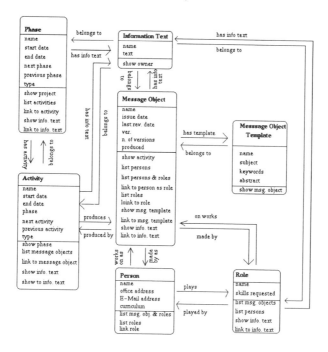

Figure 7.24: *The Coordination Data Model.* A project has phases, which are in turn decomposed into activities. People play roles as manifested by their exchange of messages. The boxes indicate entities in the system. The first subbox inside a box specifies static attributes of the entity. The second subbox gives the functions that the entity performs.

7.6   Conclusion

Two commercial development systems have been described. The courseware reuse system that was developed for *Integrated Radiological Services Limited* (IRS Ltd.) was to satisfy modest goals. This simple system, which was developed in ToolBook, includes a hypermedia library and an authoring area. The hypermedia library provides components which are created with future reusability in mind; that is, modularity and clear and extensive indexing.

One of the main insights gained from the usage of the IRS Ltd. system was that a table of contents and a media index were both useful to authors. Reusing materials from the library has provided cost benefits when assessed independently of the cost of developing the reuse library. However, many courses have to be developed from the library before the cost savings outweigh the *costs* of developing the library itself.

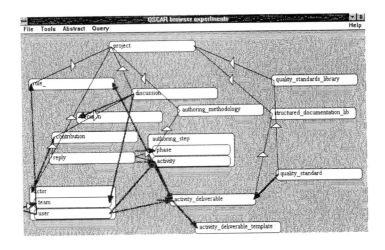

Figure 7.25: *Screen with Role*. This screen dump of the CIS shows nodes for role, actor, and other coordination-related information.

The *Open System for Collaborative Authoring and Reuse* (OSCAR) of Courseware is based on a commercial example of courseware development of multiple users over several workplaces. The system has been developed with the sponsorship of several organizations, including the aerospace courseware development company AMTECH. The system is intended to help a commercial organization be more effective in its courseware development and emphasizes the coordination of the people and the reuse of the courseware.

The OSCAR system has been implemented on *networks* of personal computers that are connected to large file servers. An object-oriented database management system stores all the information germane to the courseware development process; both the courseware itself and information about the people who develop the courseware and their methods of working. The workstations in the system are connected locally by computer networks, but distance collaboration is also supported via a satellite link.

The *architecture* of the OSCAR system may be seen as including three spaces: a common information space, a communication space, and a coauthoring space. The common information space enables people to share information relevant to the collaborative authoring process. The communication space enables the interaction and the exchange of information between members of the working group at different sites. The coauthoring space provides dedicated tools for the design and the production of multimedia courseware and contains the Coordination and Reuse Services.

The *Reuse Service* in OSCAR provides flexible access to and manipulation of courseware in the Common Information Space (CIS). The CIS contains not only the media units themselves but also other information, such as keywords, school level, and pedagogical method, which characterize the media unit. Authors can browse or search the CIS and on finding what they want can copy it and, if necessary, convert it into another format for use in new courseware.

The *Coordination Service* is based on an extensive analysis of the actually operations at AMTECH. This courseware development process is very precise and shows the importance of multiple specialists working closely together. The AME Model (which was first introduced in Chapter 2) has been used to formally represent the working processes of the courseware teams. With the existence of such a rigorous model of the process, the computer program that implements the model not only guides people in discharging their responsibilities but, at times, actually itself performs steps in the courseware development process.

The IRS Ltd. and OSCAR systems were designed specifically for courseware development. The *general principles* could be, however, applied to systems for organizations whose products are not courseware. The operations of companies that develop software or financial accounts could be precisely described and represented in the AME model. Libraries of reusable software or financial accounts could be designed and built. Instead of an 'open system for collaborative authoring and reuse' of courseware, one would then have an 'oscar' for software or an 'oscar' for financial accounts.

8
Conclusion

Childrens' story books on paper sometimes provide *interactivity*. The child moves a slip of paper in response to a question and reveals certain answers beneath the slip. Yet, neither television nor the printed page can provide the kind of creative interactivity that the computer can. With computers the message may go beyond what the printed page or other noninteractive media can convey.

The senses include the visual, auditory, tactile, and olfactory. Media for transmitting information to the senses include television, radio, printed words on paper, and audio compact disks. Like print on paper, the computer screen has in the past been a medium for communicating only text but, more recently, computers have come to life with moving images on screen and complex sounds transmitted via attached speakers. Text can be displayed at the same time, so the computer is effectively synchronizing several different media. This synchronization of multiple media is called *multimedia*.

Having different media on the computer and cleverly mixed is only the beginning of the story. The computer is an interactive device through which people can express preferences and engender a response from the computer according to that preference. With *hypermedia* the user can point to a portion of a video and change the direction of the video. For instance, pointing to the gun in the heroines' house before she is captured by the brutal heathens may activate her to use the gun to protect herself — rather as in a computer game. In fact, computer games are often excellent examples of hypermedia.

Hypermedia can be a very powerful tool for presenting educational material. Such computer-based educational material is called *courseware*. This book presents a practical methodology for development of courseware. This methodology depends on understanding how people author courseware and how courseware libraries are built.

In the design of tools to support *courseware development*, one must carefully consider the situation of the intended users and the constraints of the technology. Engineering models and the current culture of the user must be considered [118]. Many disciplines are germane to the development of courseware — from education to business to engineering to art and more — this interdisciplinary nature requires an integrative approach. Many important technological developments such as multimedia, groupware, digital libraries, and information superhighways can support courseware development.

8.1   University Problem

In the commercial sector, courseware objectives are often limited to some highly focused, practical training. In the public education system, the objectives may include the broader enlightment of the population. In this latter environment the *barriers* to the spread of educational technology are particularly salient. The American Office of Technology Assessment noted [93]:

- Lack of consistent stable funding means that prototype developments do not bring results into classrooms.
- Differing design features in the technology create barriers to diffusion. Standards would facilitate the ease with which authors and students could create and access material.

Despite many teachers being interested in courseware and the growing need to develop alternative teaching strategies, political factors also slow progress. Political factors particularly apply to universities where research has a higher status and offers greater rewards than expertise in teaching.

Extending the uptake of courseware and ensuring its high student usage is hampered by the present nature of courseware development [68]. Universities have traditionally allowed their academics a great deal of autonomy in running their courses. This trend has continued in courseware development and use. In such a laissez-faire situation computers are bought by individual departments that are often incompatible with hardware elsewhere [10].

To aid the development of good courseware a support infrastructure is required. Two schools of thought on this issue are discipline-based support versus university-wide support. *Discipline-based support* developed from the belief that a single university could not provide enough usage for any one item of courseware to justify its production. University-wide support focuses on the establishment of an infrastructure that supports all departments in one university. Discipline-based support does not have the problem of advising teachers in varying subjects, which University-based support has, but it does have difficulties reaching its clients, as the discipline-based center is likely to be far from most of them and, therefore, face-to-face communication is not practical.

A lack of communication about courseware usage between various university departments hampers the in-house development of courseware. Developers cannot draw on the strengths and experiences of their colleagues unless they know who they are. Many courseware users are keen to work in collaboration with others in producing courseware and it may be useful to setup various groups of developers, based on different criteria. A university courseware center could help coordinate a development program and publicize the work of developers, encouraging the interest of others. The Center could also coordinate technical help which could come from a computer services department.

Collaboration brings about a different attitude toward academic work in students who are able to generate ideas and who can communicate without the constraints of the teacher-pupil interchange. Managing the team work of students can be time-consuming for the teacher but information technology can facilitate the self-management of *student teams.* Furthermore, as students get involved in courseware that is presented on a network, they can augment the content of the courseware. Numerous experiences at universities have indicated that this kind of contribution from students is often the best way to get new material into the curriculum.

8.2   Courseware Life Cycle

University courseware development is often done in an ad hoc fashion. Commercial courseware development tends to be done in a rigorous fashion with well-defined intermediate products that are tested to preestablished, quality control criteria. With an understanding of this courseware life cycle, universities could improve their methods of developing courseware.

The life cycle for the development of educational hypermedia can resemble that for software. In general, there are five basic phases with each phase producing intermediate deliverables (see Figure 8.1):

1.   Analysis
2.   Design
3.   Development
4.   Implementation
5.   Evaluation

In the *analysis phase,* courseware authors analyze the learning needs of target users and define educational objectives. Then, they define course content, breadth and depth of topics, test types, and user environment [26], and construct a high-level outline of the courseware according to the educational objectives. Finally, a time schedule and estimate of costs in time and resources is proposed.

The aim of the *design phase* is to provide design specifications based on the requirements determined in the analysis phase. A mapping is established between required course content and the learning objectives. Graphics and animation needs are also specified.

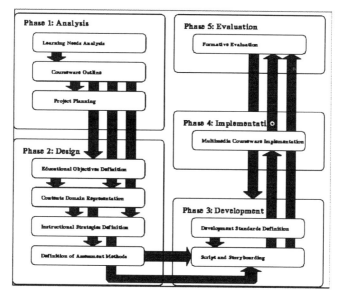

Figure 8.1: *Five Phases of Courseware Development.* Each of the 5 phases includes subphases.

The *development phase* provides guidelines for the implementation. The method for obtaining feedback is specified and flowcharts to utilize this are devised. The authors also decide whether they need to define new standards to achieve consistency, or whether they can or must use existing guidelines. At this point they are concerned about consistency in language, content, and layout. The intermediate product of this phase is the technical plan.

In the *implementation phase* a prototype version of the learning materials is produced. This prototype is further refined according to the feedback from both authors and sample users until the product is thought to contain the correct material. The intermediate product is the courseware itself. In the evaluation phase, testing and validation are performed. Testing aims to ensure that the courseware is working as intended and contains all the necessary material in the correct form.

Although it is readily understandable that *reuse* of existing courseware is desirable where possible, it is much less obvious how such activities may be undertaken. Reuse objectives are typically met by copying material from its original location, undertaking such translations as necessary to convert it into a usable format, and editing it so that it conforms to the new 'house style'. This may be a relatively painless process where the two courses follow the same instructional strategies, and are targeted at students of roughly similar capabilities, but can sometimes require almost complete rewriting where such commonality does not exist.

For all its importance, reuse of courseware is uncommon. To produce courseware within time and financial constraints further *investment* in the reuse process is merited. In the context of courseware development, reuse may be seen along the themes of organizing, retrieving, and reorganizing. First material must be collected and organized by 'librarians'. Authors can then retrieve those components that they need in creating or reorganizing material for a new course. Realizing the importance of reuse, some national government are funding the development of material that can be reused to develop courseware. For instance, the American National Library of Medicine has produced a 'visible human body' multimedia library that can be accessed on the network and from which components can be reused for educational hypermedia (see Figure 8.2).

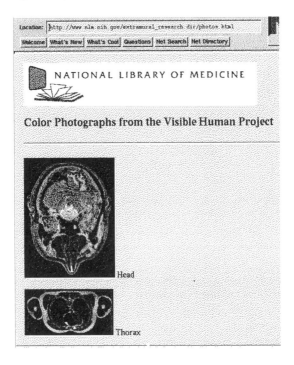

Figure 8.2: *Visible Human Body:* The window on the National Library of Medicine World Wide Web site http://www.nlm.nih.gov/extramural_research_dir/photos.html shows a small portion of the enormous archive of images of the human body that are electronically available from the Library.

The cost of constructing courseware libraries works against the economic appeal of reuse. But in the long run, reuse may be the most efficient and effective path to *courseware development*. At present reuse is often not considered until after the design is completed. Reuse should occur in every phase of courseware development, including the analysis and design phases. Reuse issues should be considered at almost every level, such as strategic planning at the organizational level, quality assurance mechanisms at the operational level, and reuse of content-related material at the authoring level.

8.3 Societal Impact

The media have an enormous influence over people's thoughts and behavior, an influence that may be set to grow massively in the new hypermedia age. Unlike the print and broadcast media, hypermedia can combine text, images and sound into a single computer-based system. This setup gives its audience more freedom to interact — to manipulate, edit, and roam (see Figure "Freeze frame"). The *impact of the new media* on society could be as great as that of television earlier this century, but if the hypermedia industry is swallowed by the international media empires, what direction will courseware take [104]?

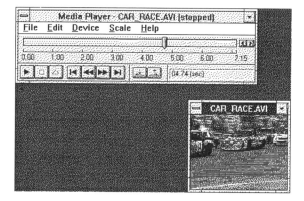

Figure 8.3: *Freeze Frame.* Microsoft Video For Windows offers standard tape transport controls, with the addition of frame-by-frame controls. Hypermedia systems give users far more freedom to interact with their medium than conventional television does.

More power and influence will accrue to those who can effectively create the messages that are delivered in the new computer-based media, but who will 'those' be? Will they be the rich and powerful — the international publishing houses, the national broadcasting corporations? Or will small groups of individuals be able to produce a message that can compete in the *marketplace* for the attention of the intended audience?

In the Soviet Union, Boris Yeltsin exerted a major effort to gain control of the country's television so that the people would hear his message. During the Romanian revolution of 1990, competing parties put their top effort into controlling that country's central *television headquarters*, even going to the length of dispatching elite tank units to capture the building.

Telephone companies, too, see the long-term importance of computer-networked media. For instance, the possibility of telephone companies transmitting television shows to the home recently became possible in the United States thanks to a relaxation of the laws that regulate the telephone companies. Promptly, the telephone companies began major mergers with cable television and entertainment companies so that they could prepare to exploit the anticipated markets. Telephone companies are spending billions of dollars building improved, optical-fiber networks for the consumer because these networks will provide the infrastructure for the new computer-networked media.

A recent survey of the British population revealed that the average Briton watches 30 hours of television per week. Some watch virtually none and some watch almost constantly, but an average person watches television more than 4 hours a day every day of the week. What do they watch? A few popular situation comedies, soap operas, crime stories, and sporting events are watched by millions. The message in these shows is hardly uplifting to the creativity of the individual, and the net effect is rather one of creating a *homogeneous set of values* in the population.

The printed word remains a medium that is often used to advance *freedom.* Books and other printed products are often accessed and read by small audiences for whom the publication is a significant source of information and direction. An individual is able to produce a written document that is targeted to a few people.

The creation of hypermedia is not easily done by an individual. An individual might sit alone in the bedroom night after night and eventually produce a brilliant novel. But the production of hypermedia may entail a plot fashioned by a single author combined with the production of video by a crew of camera experts, actors, costume designers, and sound track specialists. And the interactive part of hypermedia may require computing skills that relatively few people have. The management of the *team* of people who might create educational hypermedia is itself a major job.

The Many Using and Creating Hypermedia (MUCH) system and the Open System for Collaborative Authoring and Reuse (OSCAR) help groups produce hypermedia. They contain *computerized manuals* that include job descriptions and production schedules which staff can use to guide their work. Additionally, they provide the framework for a reuse library.

With the methodologies and tools which MUCH and OSCAR provide, groups may become more skilled in the production of courseware and begin to do in this arena what a solo author has long been able to do in the realm of the printed word. There might develop *regions of a country* that become particularly proficient at using tools like MUCH and OSCAR, at building reuse libraries, and at producing courseware to serve diverse interests.

Courseware is used by only a small fraction of teachers today. Although the expectation is that this fraction will grow and grow, the factors that influence this growth are many and varied. This book has argued that critical factors in courseware development are *coordination* and reuse. These who exploit the new methods and tools for courseware development should be in an improved position to significantly contribute to education.

References

1. Alessi, S M and Trollip, S R, *Computer-Based Instruction, Methods and Development*, Prentice Hall, Englewood Cliffs, New Jersey, 1985.

2. Alty, James L, "Multimedia - What Is It and How Do We Exploit It?," *Proceedings of the HCI '91 Conference: People and Computers VI*, pp. 31-44, Wiley, 1991.

3. Annis, P, *Use of Telephones and Computers in The Classroom at Boston University*, 1992. (this work was distributed electronicaly to various newsgroups in 1992, copy can be obtained from the author at email address annis@crca.bu.edu)

4. Avner, A, "Production of Computer-Based Instructional Materials," in *Issues in Instructional Systems Development*, ed. H F O'Neil, Jr, pp. 133-180, Academic Press, New York, 1979.

5. Bannon, L, Bjorn-Andersen, N, and Due-Thomsen, B, "Computer Support for Cooperative Work: An Appraisal and Critique," in *Eurinfo '88. Information Systems for Orgnizational Effectiveness*, ed. H.J. Bullinger, Nortl, Amsterdam, Holland, 1988.

6. Bannon, L J and Schmidt, K, "CSCW: Four Characters in Search of a Context," *Proceedings of the 1st European Conference on Computer Supported Cooperative Work*, pp. 358-372, Computer Sciences House, Slough, England, 1989.

7. Barker, P G, *Author Languages for CAL*, MacMillan Education, Basingstoke, 1987.

8. Barnsley, M, "SMARTbook," *BSC Computer Bulletin*, Frax Ltd., Aberdeen, England, February, 1994.

9. Berners-Lee, Tim, Cailliau, Robert, Luotonen, Ari, Nielsen, Henrik Frystyk, and Secret, Arthur, "The World Wide Web," *Communications of the ACM*, vol. 37, no. 8, pp. 76-82, August 1994.

10. Bidin, A R H and Drabble, G, "An Organisational Approach Towards The Development of Educational Computing in a University Environment," *Computer Education*, vol. 14, no. 137, 1990.

11. Bieber, Michael, "Issues in Modeling a Dynamic Hypertext Interface for Non-Hypertext Systems," *Hypertext '91 Proceedings*, pp. 203-218, ACM Press, New York, 1991.

12. Bloom, B S, *Taxonomy of Educational Objectives: The Classification of Educational Goals,* Longman, London, 1956.

13. Boeing Company, IBM Federal Systems Company, and Unisys Corporation, "STARS Conceptual Framework for Reuse Processes (CFRP)," *Volume 1: Definition, Version 3.0*, United States Air Force, Hanscom Air Force Base,

Massachusetts, October 25, 1993.

14. Bolt, R, "Put-That-There: Voice and Gesture at the Graphics Interface," *ACM Computer Graphics*, vol. 14, no. 3, pp. 262-270, July 1980.

15. Borenstein, N S and Thyberg, C A, "Power, Ease of Use, and Cooperative Work in a Practical Multimedia Message System," *International Journal of Man Machine Studies*, vol. 34, no. 2, pp. 229-259, 1991.

16. Bourdeau, J, "Automating Instructional Planning," in *NATO ASI - Automating Instructional Design, Development and Delivery*, ed. R D Tennysons, Springer-Verlag, Heidelberg, 1993.

17. Brunson, S, "CAI Frame by Frame," *TechTrends*, vol. 30, no. 4, pp. 24-25, 1985.

18. Buford, John F Koegel, "Architectures and Issues for Distributed Multimedia Systems," in *Multimedia Systems*, ed. John F Koegel Buford, pp. 45-63, ACM Press, New York, 1994.

19. Burton, B A, Aragon, R W, Bailey, S A, and Koehler, K D, "The Reusable Software Library," *IEEE Software*, vol. 4, pp. 25-33, 1987.

20. Caroll, S J and Tosi, H J, *Management by Objectives,* MacMillan, New York, 1973.

21. Cartwright, D and Zander, A, *Group Dynamics: Research and Theory,* Harper and Row, New York, 1968.

22. Charnock, Elizabeth, Rada, Roy, Stichler, Steve, and Weygant, Peter, "A Rule-Based Task-Oriented Method of Creating Usable Hypertext for Commercial Audiences," *Interacting with Computers*, vol. 6, no. 3, pp. 275-287, September 1994.

23. Chen, Chaomei, Rada, Roy, and Zeb, Akmal, "An Extended Fisheye View Browser for Collaborative Writing," *International Journal of Human-Computer Studies, 40*, pp. 859-878, 1994.

24. Chignell, Mark H, Nordhausen, Bernd, Valdez, J Felix, and Waterworth, John A, "The HEFTI Model of Text to Hypertext Conversion," *Hypermedia*, vol. 3, no. 3, pp. 187-205, 1991.

25. Cleynenbrengel, J Van, Bellon, E, Marchal, G, and Suetens, P, "Design and Evaluation of a Demonstrator for Radiological Multimedia Communication," in *Medical Multimedia*, ed. Roy Rada and Claude Ghaoui, pp. 24-41, Intellect Books, Oxford, England, 1995.

26. Clifton, Chris, "Intelligent Training System using Hypermedia," Technical Report, Logica Cambridge Limited, Cambridge, England, 1989.

27. Corvetta, A, Pomponio, G, Salvi, A, and Luchetti, M M, "Teaching Medicine Using Hypertext: Three Years of Experience at the Ancona Medical School," *Artificial Intelligence in Medicine*, vol. 3, pp. 203-209, 1991.

28. Cybulski, Jacob L and Reed, Karl, "A Hypertext Based Software Engineering Environment," *IEEE Software*, vol. 9, no. 2, pp. 62-68, 1992.

29. Dalton, R, "Group-Writing Tools: Four That Connect," *Information Week*, pp. 62-65, March 9, 1987.

30. Davies, H, Hall, W, Heath, I, Hill, G, and Wilkins, R, "Microcosm: An Open Hypermedia Environment for Information Interchange," *Proceedings of European Conference on Hypertext '92*, pp. 181-190, ACM Press, New York, 1992.

31. Diaper, Dan and Addison, Mark, "Task Analysis and Systems Analysis for Software Development," *Interacting with Computers*, vol. 4, no. 1, pp. 124-139, 1992.

32. Diaz, L, "PathMAC: An Alternative Approach to Medical School Education at Cornell School of Medicine," in *Hypertext/Hypermedia Handbook*, ed. E Berk and J Devlin, pp. 488-492, McGraw-Hill, New York, 1991.

33. DISA/CIM Software Reuse Program, *Domain Analysis and Design Process, Version 1 Technical Report 1222-04-210/301.1*, Defense Information Systems Agency Center for Information Management, Arlington, Virginia, 1993.

34. DoD Software Reuse Initiative, *DoD Software Reuse Vision and Strategy. Technical Report 1222-04-210/40*, Center for Software Reuse Operations, Alexandria, Virginia, 1992.

35. Egan, D E, Remde, J R, Gomez, L M, Landauer, T K, Eberhardt, J, and Lochbaum, C C, "Formative Design-Evaluation of 'SuperBook'," *ACM Transactions of Informatioiyan Systems*, vol. 7, no. 1, pp. 30-57, 1989.

36. Engelbart, D C and W, English, "A Research Center for Augmenting Human Intellect," *Proceedings of the Fall Joint Computer Conference*, vol. 33, pp. 395-410, AFIPS Press, Montvale, New Jersey, 1968.

37. Frakes, W B and Gandel, P B, "Representing Reusable Software," *Information Software Technology*, vol. 32, no. 10, pp. 653-664, December, 1990.

38. Franks, John, *WN Server*, http://hopf.math.nwu.edu/docs/overview.html, john@math.nwu.edu, 1995.

39. Fujikawa, M, "CD-ROM: Present State, Future Prospect, and Problems.," *2nd International Conference on the Effective Use of CD-ROM Databases*, pp. 3-18, ISACO, Japan, 1990.

40. Furnas, George, "Generalized Fisheye Views," *CHI'86 Proceedings*, pp. 16-23, ACM Press, New York, 1986.

41. Gaines, B R and Malcolm, N, "Supporting Collaboration in Digital Journal Production," *Journal of Organizational Computing*, vol. 3, no. 2, pp. 195-213, 1993.

42. Goldman-Segall, R, "Interpreting Video Data: Introducing a 'Significance Measure' to Layer Descriptions," *Journal of Educational Multimedia and*

Hypermedia, vol. 2, no. 3, pp. 261-281, 1993.

43. Goodenow, Ronald K and Carpenter, Sam K, "Designing and Implementing a Rural Telemedicine Project: Issues and Learnings," in *Medical Multimedia*, ed. Roy Rada and Claude Ghaoui, pp. 53-69, Intellect Books, Oxford, England, 1995.

44. Goodman, S E, Press, L I, Ruth, S R, and Ruthowski, A M, "The Global Diffusion of the Internet: Patterns and Problems," *Communications of the ACM*, vol. 37, no. 8, pp. 27-31, August 1994.

45. Gouma, P, Deakin, A G, White, B, and Rada, R, "A Study of the Evolution of a University Research Department Facilitated by a Groupware System (MUCH)," *Journal of Intelligent Systems*, 1994.

46. Grabinger, R S, "CRT Text Design: Psychological Attributes Underlying The Evaluation of Models of CRT Text Displays," *Journal of Visual and Verbal Languaging*, vol. 4, no. 1, pp. 17-39, 1984.

47. Green, James L, "The Evolution of DVI System Software," *Communications of the ACM*, vol. 35, no. 1, pp. 52-67, 1992.

48. Griss, M L, "Software Reuse: From Library to Factory," *IBM Systems Journal*, vol. 32, no. 4, pp. 548-566, 1993.

49. Grudin, J, "CSCW: The Convergence of Two Disciplines," *ACM SIGCHI Conference on Human Factors in Computing Systems*, pp. 91-98, ACM Press, New York, 1991.

50. GTE Government, *NATO Standard for Development of Reusable Software Components*, NATO Communications and Information Systems Agency, Brussels, Belgium, March 1992.

51. GTE Government, *NATO Standard for Management of a Reusable Software Component Library*, NATO Communications and Information Systems Agency, Brussels, Belgium, March 1992.

52. GTE Government, *NATO Standard for Software Reuse Procedures*, NATO Communications and Information Systems Agency, Brussels, Belgium, March 1992.

53. Hahn, Harley and Stout, Rick, *The Internet Complete Reference*, McGraw-Hill, Berkeley, California, 1994.

54. Halasz, Frank and Schwartz, Mayer, "The Dexter hypertext reference model," *Proceedings of The Hypertext Standardization Workshop*, pp. 95-134, U.S Government Printing Office, Washington, DC, 1990.

55. Halasz, Frank and Schwartz, Mayer, "The Dexter Hypertext Reference Model," *Communications of the ACM*, pp. 30-39, ACM Press, New York, 1994.

56. Hammond, N and Allinson, L, "Extending Hypertext for Learning: An Investigation of Access and Guiding Tools," *Proceedings BSC HCI '89*, Nottingham,

UK, 1989.

57. Hansen, Wilfred J and Haas, Christina, "Reading and Writing with Computers: A Framework for Explaining Differences in Performance," *Communications of the ACM*, vol. 31, no. 9, pp. 1080-1089, September 1988.

58. Hardman, Lynda, "Hypertext Tips: Experiences in Developing a Hypertext Tutorial," *Proceedings of People and Computers IV*, pp. 437-451, Cambridge University Press, Cambridge, U.K., 1988.

59. Hardman, Lynda, Bulterman, Dick C A, and Rossum, Guida van, "The Amsterdam Hypermedia Model: Adding Time and Context to the Dexter Model," *Communications of the ACM*, vol. 37, no. 2, pp. 50-62, February 1994.

60. Hathaway, M, "Variables of Computer Screen Display and How They Affect Learning," *Educational Technology*, vol. 24, no. 1, pp. 7-10, 1984.

61. Hiltz, S R and Turoff, M, *The Network Nation: Human Communication via Computer,* Addison-Wesley, Reading, Massachusetts, 1993.

62. Hoffman, L R, "Group Problem Solving," in *Group Processes*, ed. L Berkowitz, pp. 67-100, Academic Press, New York, 1978.

63. Holibaugh, Robert R, Cohen, Sholom G, Kang, Kyo C, and Peterson, Spencer, "Reuse Where to Begin and Why," *Proceedings of Tri-Ada'89*, pp. 266-277, ACM Press, New York, 1989.

64. IMSL, *Library User's Manual 1.0 Edition,* IMSL Math, Houston, Texas, 1987.

65. Intel, "The Audio Video Kernel: The Foundation for a Portable, Extendable Multimedia Environment," *White Paper*, Multiteq Ltd, Aylesbury, England, October 1992.

66. International Standards Organization, *Information Processing - Text and Office Systems - Standard Generalized Markup Language (SGML),* ISO 8879, Geneva, 1988.

67. International Standards Organization, *Information Technology - Hypermedia/Time-based Structuring Language (HyTime),* ISO 10744, 1991.

68. James, E B, "Computer-Based Teaching for Undergraduates: Old Problems and New Possibilities," *Computer Education*, vol. 10, no. 267, 1986.

69. Johnson-Lenz, P and Johnson-Lenz, T, "Post-Mechanistic Groupware Primitives: Rhythms, Boundaries and Containers," *International Journal of Man Machine Studies*, vol. 34, no. 3, pp. 385-418, 1991.

70. Kearsley, G, "Authoring Tools: An Introduction," *Journal of Computer-Based Instruction*, vol. 11, no. 3, p. 67, 1984.

71. King, N and Anderson, N, "Innovation in Working Groups," in *Innovation and creativity at work*, ed. M.A. West and J.L. Farr, John Wiley & Sons Ltd, Chichester, England, 1990.

72. Kling, R, "Cooperation, Coordination and Control in Computer-Supported Work," *Communications of the ACM*, vol. 34, no. 2, pp. 83-88, 1991.

73. Krol, Ed, *The Whole Internet: User's Guide and Catalog*, O'Reilly & Associates, Sebastopol, California, 1992.

74. Landow, G P, "Hypertext and Collaborative Work: The Example of Intermedia," in *Intellectual Teamwork: Social Foundations of Cooperative Work*, ed. J Galegher, R E Kraut, and C Egido, pp. 407-428, Lawrence Erlbaum Associates, Hillsdale, New Jersey, 1990.

75. Lange, D, "A Formal Model for Hypertext," *Proceedings of the Hypertext Standardization Workshop (National Institute of Standards and Technology Special Publication 500-178)*, pp. 145-166, U.S Government Printing Office, Washington DC, 1990.

76. Leiner, Barry, "Internet Technology," *Communications of the ACM*, vol. 37, no. 8, p. 32, August 1994.

77. Little, Thomas D, "Time-Based Media Representation and Delivery," in *Multimedia Systems*, ed. John F Koegel Buford, pp. 175-200, ACM Press, New York, 1994.

78. Malone, Thomas and Crowston, Kevin, "What is Coordination Theory and How Can it Help Design Cooperative Work Systems?," *Proceedings of the Conference on Computer-Supported Cooperative Work*, pp. 357-370, ACM Press, New York, 1990.

79. McDonough, Denise, Strivens, Janet, and Rada, Roy, "University Courseware Development: Differences Between Computer-Based Teaching Users and Non-Users," *Computers and Education,*, vol. 23, no. 3, pp. 211-220, 1994.

80. McKnight, Cliff, Dillon, Andrew, and Richardson, John, "A Comparison of Linear and Hypertext Formats in Information Retrieval," in *Hypertext: State of the Art*, ed. R McAleese and C Green, pp. 10-19, Intellect Limited, Oxford, 1990.

81. Merrill, M D, "Where is The Authoring in Authoring Systems?," *Journal of Computer-Based Instruction*, vol. 12, pp. 90-96, 1985.

82. Meyer, B, "Reusability: The Case for Object-Oriented Design," *IEEE Software*, pp. 50-64, March 1987.

83. Mili, Hafedh and Rada, Roy, "Medical Expertext as Regularity in Semantic Nets," *Artificial Intelligence in Medicine*, vol. 2, no. 4, pp. 217-229, 1990.

84. MIT Athena, *http://web.mit.edu/afs/.athena/astaff/project/logos/olh/welcome*, Cambridge, Massachusetts, January 1995.

85. Nass, Richard, "Competitive Video Compression-Decompression Schemes Forge Ahead," *Electronic Design*, pp. 82-90, June 1994.

86. National Library and Information Associations Council, *Guidelines for Thesaurus Structure, Construction, and Use,* American National Standards Institute, New York, 1980.

87. Neuwirth, Christine and Kaufer, David, "The Role of External Representations in the Writing Process: Implications for the Design of Hypertext-based Writing Tools," *Proceedings Hypertext '89,* pp. 343-364, ACM Press, New York, 1989.

88. Newcomb, Steven R, Kipp, Neill A, and Newcomb, Victoria T, "The HyTime Hypermedia/Time-based Document Structuring Language," *Communications of the ACM,* vol. 34, no. 11, pp. 67-83, 1991.

89. Nielsen, Jacob, *Hypertext and Hypermedia,* Academic Press, New York, 1990.

90. Nielsen, Jakob, "The Art of Navigating Through Hypertext," *Communications of the ACM,,* vol. 33, no. 3, pp. 296-310, 1990.

91. Nunamaker, J F, Kennis, A R, Valacich, J S, Vogel, D R, and George, J F, "Electronic Meeting Systems to Support Group Work," *Communications of the ACM,* vol. 34, no. 7, pp. 40-61, July, 1991.

92. Nyce, James M and Kahn, Paul, "Innovation, Pragmaticism, and Technological Continuity: Vannevar Bush's Memex," *Journal American Society Information Science,* vol. 40, no. 3, pp. 214-220, 1989.

93. Office of Technology Assessment, *Power On!: New Tools for Teaching and Learning,* Congress of the US, Office of Technology, Washington, D.C., 1988.

94. O'Neil Jr., H F and Paris, J., *Computer Based Instruction: A State of the Art Assessment,* Academic Press, London, England, 1981.

95. Oppenheim, C, "CD-ROM: An Introduction to the Technology and its Potential Applications," *Proceedings on Advanced Information Systems - AiS '91,* pp. 69-75, 1991.

96. Orlansky, J and String, J, *Cost Effectiveness of Computer-Based Instruction in Military Training,* Institute for Defence Analysis, Arlington, Virginia, 1978.

97. Papert, S, *Mindstorms,* Basic Books, New York, 1980.

98. Pentland, A, Picard, R, Davenport, G, and Welsh, R, "The BT/MIT Project on Advanced Image Tools for Telecommunications: an Overview," *Proceedings of 2nd International Conference on Image Communications,* 1993.

99. Persico, D, Sarti, L, and Viarengo, "Browsing a Database of Multimedia Learning Material," *Interactive Learning International,* vol. 8, pp. 213-235, 1992.

100. Phillips, W A, "Individual Author Prototyping: Desktop Development of Courseware.," *Computers and Education,* vol. 14, no. 9, 1990.

101. Platt, S, *TEAMS: A Game to Develop Group Skills,* Gower Publishing Company, Aldershot, England, 1989.

102. Quarterman, J S, *The Matrix: Computer Networks and Conferencing Systems Worldwide,* Digital Press, Bedford, Massachusetts, 1990.

103. Rada, R, Deakin, A, and Beer, M, "Collaborative Development of Courseware: Part One - Examples," *Journal of Intelligent Tutoring Media*, vol. 4, no. 2, pp. 69-77, 1993.

104. Rada, R, "Multimedia or Slavery?," *Science for Public Advancement*, pp. 13-15, Winter, 1993.

105. Rada, Roy, Keith, Barbara, Burgoine, Marc, George, Steven, and Reid, David, "Collaborative Writing of Text and Hypertext," *Hypermedia*, vol. 1, no. 2, pp. 93-110, 1989.

106. Rada, Roy, Mili, Hafedh, Bicknell, Ellen, and Blettner, Maria, "Development and Application of a Metric on Semantic Nets," *IEEE Transactions on Systems, Man, and Cybernetics*, vol. 19, no. 1, pp. 17-30, 1989.

107. Rada, Roy, "Guidelines for Multiple Users Creating Hypertext: SQL and HyperCard Experiments," in *Computers and Writing: Models and Tools*, ed. Patrik Holt and Noel Williams, pp. 61-89, Blackwell/Ablex Publishing, Norwood, New Jersey, 1989.

108. Rada, Roy, "Hypertext Writing and Document Reuse: the Role of a Semantic Net," *Electronic Publishing*, vol. 3, no. 3, pp. 3-13, 1990.

109. Rada, Roy, *Hypertext: from Text to Expertext,* McGraw-Hill, London, 1991.

110. Rada, Roy, Zeb, Akmal, You, Geeng-Neng, Michailidis, Antonios, and Mhashi, Mahmoud, "Collaborative Hypertext and the MUCH System," *Journal Information Science: Principles & Practice*, vol. 17, pp. 191-1968, 1991.

111. Rada, Roy and Murphy, Clare, "Searching versus Browsing in Hypertext," *Hypermedia*, vol. 4, no. 1, pp. 1-30, 1992.

112. Rada, Roy and Carson, George S, "Standards: the New Media," *Communications of the ACM*, vol. 37, no. 9, pp. 23-25, 1994.

113. Rada, Roy and Ramsey, Phillip, *ACM SIGBIO CD-ROM Medical Multimedia & Informatics,* ACM Press, New York, 1994.

114. Rada, Roy and Ramsey, Phillip, *ACM SIGBIO Newsletter, 14, 3,* ACM Press, New York, December 1994.

115. Rada, Roy, *Interactive Media,* Springer-Verlag, New York, 1995.

116. Ragsdale, Ronald G, *Evaluation of Microcomputer Courseware,* Ontario Institute for Studies in Education Press, Toronto, Canada, 1982.

117. Ramamoorthy, C V, Garg, V, and Prakash, A, "Support for Reusabiltiy in Genesis," *IEEE Transactions on Software Engineering*, vol. 14, pp. 1145-1154, 1988.

118. Rasmussen, Jens, Pejtersen, Annelise Mark, and Schmidt, Kjeld, "Taxonomy of Cognitive Work Analysis," *Riso-M-2871*, Riso National Laboratory, Roskilde, Denmark, 1990.

119. Rein, G L, Ellis, C A, and Berkow, Robert, "The Merck Manual of Diagnosis and Therapy, 16th Edition," *International Journal of Man Machine Studies*, vol.

34 &N 3, pp. 349-368, Merck, Rahway, New Jersey, 1992.

120. Roblyer, M D, "Instructional Design Versus Authoring of Courseware: Some Crucial Differences," *AEDS Journal*, vol. 14, no. 4, pp. 173-181, 1981.

121. Rodden, T, "A Survey of CSCW Systems," *Interacting with Computers*, vol. 3, no. 2, pp. 319-353, 1991.

122. Rossum, G van, Jansen, J, Mullender, K S, and Bulterman, D C A, "CMIFed: A Presentation Environment for Portable Hypermedia Documents," *Proceedings of the First ACM International Conference on Multimedia*, pp. 183-188, ACM Press, New York, August 1993.

123. Scardamalia, Marlene and Bereiter, Carl, "Knowledge Telling and Knowledge Transforming in Written Composition," in *Advances in Applied Psycholinguistics*, ed. Sheldon Rosenberg, pp. 142-175, Cambridge University Press, Cambridge, England, 1987.

124. Schmidt, K, "Riding a Tiger, or Computer Supported Cooperative Work," *Proceedings of the Second European Conference on Computer-Supported Cooperative Work*, pp. 1-16, Kluwer, Amsterdam, September 17-25, 1991.

125. Self, J, *Microcomputers in Education: A Critical Appraisal of Educational Software.*, The Harvester Press Publishing Group, Brighton, England, 1985.

126. Senge, P M, *The Fifth Discipline*, Doubleday/Currency, New York, 1990.

127. Shackelford, Russell L, "Educational Computing: Myths versus Methods -Why Computers Haven't Helped and What We Can Do about It," *Proceedings of the Conference on Computers and the Quality of Life*, pp. 139-146, The George Washington University, Washington, DC, 1990.

128. Shannon, Claude and Weaver, W, *The Mathematical Theory of Communication*, University of Illinois Press, Urbana, Illinois, 1949.

129. Sharples, M, Goodlet, J S, Beck, E E, Wood, C C, Easterbrook, S M, and Plowma, L, "Research Issues in the Study of Computer Supported Collaborative Writing," in *Computer Supported Collaborative Writing*, ed. M Sharples, Springer-Verlag, London, 1993.

130. Shepherd, A, "Analysis and Training in Information Technology Tasks," in *Task Analysis for Human-Computer Interaction*, ed. D Diaper, Ellis-Horwood, Chichester, England, 1989.

131. Shneiderman, Ben and Kearsley, Greg, *Hypertext Hands-On!*, Addison-Wesley, Reading, Massachusetts, 1989.

132. Siegel, J, Dubrovsky, V, Kiesler, S, and McGuire, T W, "Group Processes in Computer-Mediated Communication," *Organizational Behavior and Human Decision Processes*, vol. 37, pp. 157-187, 1986.

133. Sivitier, P, *The CAL for Computing Project*, Proceedings Conference on Computers and Hypermedia in Engineering Education, SEFI Vaasa Institute of

Technology, Vaasa, 1993.

134. Smith, H T, Hannessy, P A, and Lunt, G A, "The Activity Model Environment: An Object-Oriented Framework for Describing Organisational Communication," *Proceedings of the lst European Conference on Computer-Supported Cooperative Work,* pp. 160-172, Computer Sciences House, Slough, U.K., 1989.

135. Software Technology for Adaptable Reliable Systems (STARS), *The Reuse-Oriented Software Evolution (ROSE) Process Model, Version 0.5. Unisys STARS Technical Report STARS-UC-05155/001/00,* Advanced Research Projects Agency, STARS Technology Center, Arlington, Virginia, July, 1993.

136. Software Technology for Adaptable Reliable Systems (STARS), "Organization Domain Modelling (ODM) Volume I - Conceptual Foundations, Process and Workproduct Descriptions, Version 0.5 - DRAFT.," *Unisys STARS Technical Report STARS-UC-05156/024/00,* Advanced Research Projects Agency, STARS Technology Center, Arlington, Virginia, July, 1993.

137. Stewart, V, *Change: The challenge of management,* McGraw-Hill, New York, 1983.

138. Strawn, John, "Digital Audio Representation and Processing," in *Multimedia Systems,* ed. John F Koegel Buford, pp. 65-108, ACM Press, New York, 1994.

139. Suppes, P, "The Users of Computers in Education," *Scientific American,* vol. 215, pp. 207-220, 1966.

140. Tiro, J R and Gregorius, H, "Management of Reuse at IBM," *IBM Systems Journal,* vol. 32R, no. 4, pp. 612-615, 1993.

141. Trainor, R, "Computers, Arts Based Teaching and Rising Student Numbers," *CTISS File,* vol. 13, pp. 3-6, 1992.

142. US Market Intelligence Research Company, *Software World,* vol. 21, no. 4, p. 9, 1987.

143. Vaughan, Tay, *MultiMedia: Making it Work,* McGraw-Hill, New York, 1993.

144. Virginia Center of Excellence for Software Reuse and Technology Transfer, *Reuse Adoption Guidebook. Technical Report SPC-92051-CMC,* Software Productivity Consortium, Herndon, Virginia, November, 1992.

145. Wager, W, "Design Considerations for Instructional Computing Programs," *Journal of Educational Technology Systems,* vol. 10, no. 3, pp. 261-269, 1982.

146. Wasmund, M, "Implementing Critical Success Factors in Software Reuse," *IBM Systems Journal,* vol. 32, no. 4, pp. 595-611, 1993.

147. Wenger, E, *Artificial Intelligence and Tutoring Systems- Computational and Cognitive Approaches to the Communication of knowledge,* Morgan Kaufmann Publishers, San Francisco, 1987.

148. Williams, P J and Hammond, P, "The Creation of Electronic Visual Archives for Teaching and Learning," *Proceedings of the 12th UK Eurographics*

Conference, 1994.

149. Wilson, D, "Wrestling with multimedia standards," *Computer Design*, vol. 31, no. 1, pp. 70-88, 1992.

150. Wilson, P, "Computer-Supported Cooperative Work (CSCW) - Origins, Concepts and Research Initiatives," *Computer Networks and ISDN Systems*, vol. 23, no. 1-3, pp. 91-95, 1991.

151. Wright, Patricia, "Manual Dexterity: A User-Oriented Approach to Creating Computer Documentation," *Proceedings of CHI '83*, pp. 11-18, ACM Press, New York, 1983.

Index